OSPREY AIRCRAFT OF THE ACES • 112

Fokker D.XXI Aces of World War 2

SERIES EDITOR: TONY HOLMES

OSPREY AIRCRAFT OF THE ACES • 112

Fokker D.XXI Aces of World War 2

Kari Stenman and Peter de Jong

OSPREY
PUBLISHING

Front Cover
During the morning of 6 January 1940, 17 Ilyushin DB-3M bombers of 6th DBAP took off from their base at Kretchevitsy, east of Lake Peipusjärvi, and headed for the Kuopio ammunition factory complex in central eastern Finland. The first division of nine DB-3Ms flew directly to the target, dropped its bombs and returned to base without meeting opposition. The second division of eight aircraft drifted too far east, pushed by the wind, and crossed the coast of the Gulf of Finland just south of Utti, which was then the Finnish Air Force's main Fokker D.XXI base.

As the bombers headed to the target, 1Lt Per-Erik Sovelius of 4/LLv 24, who was flying D.XXI FR-92 to Utti from Lappeenranta, intercepted the DB-3Ms and shot one of them down. The remaining seven bombed Kuopio as planned before returning by the same route they had come, south along the railway line.

By now 1Lt Jorma Sarvanto had scrambled alone from Utti in FR-97, his wingman failing to get the engine in his Fokker started. Sarvanto received continuous information on the location of the Soviet bombers by radio until he engaged them near Utti at 1204 hrs. In just four minutes he shot down six DB-3Ms, including the lead aeroplane of Maj Maistrenko. Most of the bombers caught fire after a few bursts from Sarvanto's four 7.7 mm machine guns. All of the aircraft crashed 28 km (17 miles) south of Utti. When the Finnish fighter pilots inspected the wrecks they noted that the bombers lacked self-sealing fuel tanks and fire extinguishers.

Sarvanto had also come under enemy fire during the one-sided attack, and 23 bullet holes were counted in his aeroplane, requiring it to be flown to the State Aircraft Factory for full inspection and eventual repair.

Thanks to his outstanding marksmanship, 1Lt Jorma Sarvanto had become the first pilot to achieve 'ace-in-a-mission' status in World War 2, and his feat aroused huge interest in the world's press (*Cover artwork by Mark Postlethwaite*)

Title Verso Page
D.XXIs FR-94, -95 and -86 of LeR 1 are seen here lined up for a parade held at Suur-Merijoki on 16 May 1939. Six months after this photograph was taken they were serving in the frontline with LLv 24. The men saluting are, from left to right, LLv 12 commander Maj A Nisonen, regiment commander Col Y Opas, LLv 14 commander Maj J Moilanen and LLv 10 commander Maj K Janarmo (*Finnish Air Force*)

First published in Great Britain in 2013 by Osprey Publishing
Midland House, West Way, Botley, Oxford, OX2 0PH
43-01 21st Street, Suite 220B, Long Island City, NY, 11101, USA

E-mail; info@ospreypublishing.com

Osprey Publishing is part of the Osprey Group

A CIP catalogue record for this book is available from the British Library
ISBN: 978 1 78096 062 3
PDF e-book ISBN: 978 1 78096 063 0
e-Pub ISBN: 978 1 78096 064 7

Edited by Tony Holmes and Philip Jarrett
Cover Artwork by Mark Postlethwaite
Aircraft Profiles by Chris Davey
Index by Michael Forder
Originated by PDQ Digital Media Solutions, UK
Printed in China through Bookbuilders

13 14 15 16 17 10 9 8 7 6 5 4 3 2 1

Osprey Publishing is supporting the Woodland Trust, the UK's leading woodland conservation charity, by funding the dedication of trees.

www.ospreypublishing.com

ACKNOWLEDGEMENTS
The authors wish to record their gratitude to the following Fokker D.XXI pilots who have given of their time in answering queries and presenting accounts for inclusion in this volume – the late Lt Col Aulis Bremer, the late Gen Maj Gustaf Magnusson, the late WO Ilmari Juutilainen, the late Maj Martti Kalima, the late Col Jorma Karhunen, the late Maj Veikko Karu, the late Lt Col Jorma Sarvanto and Sgt Guus Kiel. Thanks also go to Frits Gerdessen for his research and interviews with now-deceased pilots, and to Pieter Hooijmans for his assistance in assessing Dutch aerial victory claims from May 1940.

CONTENTS

ORIGINS

The Fokker D.XXI was obviously not one of the great fighters of World War 2, but for three minor neutral nations, Holland, Denmark and Finland, it was the nearest thing they had to the Supermarine Spitfire when they were invaded by the totalitarian juggernauts of Nazi Germany and Soviet Russia. Thanks largely to the Finnish pilots' first-class training, the D.XXI, rather unexpectedly, shone like a polar star during the gruesome winter of war in 1939-40.

The fighter that had its 'finest hour' in that vicious northern winter was originally intended for service in a very different environment, namely the tropical heat of the Netherlands East Indies (now Indonesia). Anthony Fokker, the company's founder, had been born in the colony in 1890, but grew up in Holland and built his first aeroplanes in Germany. The outbreak of World War 1 saw Fokker evolve into a major supplier of fighter aircraft to the Kaiser's army, noteworthy designs being the Fokker Eindecker monoplanes, the Dr I triplane and the D VII biplane.

Subsequently based in Amsterdam and New York, Fokker enjoyed renewed success with both airliners and military aircraft during the 1920s. However, Anthony himself loathed scientific research and long-term investment. This meant that by 1934 his trademark mixed construction of fabric-covered steel-tube fuselages and wooden wings was obsolete, and his company was only a shadow of its former self, major export markets having dried up.

In May 1934 the Netherlands East Indies Army (NEIA) issued a requirement for a new fighter, demanding a 410 km/h (255 mph) top speed, with a fixed undercarriage and wood and metal construction for maintenance reasons. Armament was to comprise one fuselage-mounted heavy machine gun and two light machine guns in the wings that were to be adjustable through ten degrees upwards and sideways, although this latter requirement was eventually dropped.

A derivative of Fokker's elegant D.XVII biplane fighter, designated D.XIX, was dropped in favour of the low-wing *Ontwerp* (Design) 112. Development of the new monoplane was led by the company's new chief designer, Erich Schatzki, a former Junkers and Lufthansa engineer who was Jewish and had fled Hitler's Germany. Inline-engined sleek-fuselage variants were studied, Fokker showing considerable interest in the *moteur-canon* Hispano-Suiza 12Y

The first three men to fly the D.XXI pose in front of the prototype after its maiden flight. NEIA Capt Van Lent shakes the hand of veteran factory pilot Emil Meinecke, while to the left of them is Fokker's chief constructor, Erich Schatzki, who had never designed or flown fighters before, but did fly his own brainchild. On the right is Fokker flight-test engineer Frans Stok. The wheel fairings and a cockpit canopy were not fitted for the first flight (*T Postma*)

The prototype arrives at the Fokker flight-test department at Schiphol Airport on 16 March 1936, initial testing having taken place at Eindhoven. The scene must have been similar on 1 May, when a new pilot barely managed to land the aircraft after making a mess of a spin test – the rudder was soon enlarged to improve spin recovery. The prototype wore full NEIA markings and the serial FD-322 (*T Postma*)

engine, but the customer preferred an air-cooled radial. Stipulating the Bristol Mercury, the NEIA cabled its approval of 'type D two one', as the new fighter had, meanwhile, been designated, on 1 April 1935. Fokker was inconsistent in its 1935 abandonment of Roman numerals in its designations, and the D.21 is better known internationally as the D.XXI.

Owing to soggy conditions at Amsterdam's Schiphol Airport, the prototype, powered by a 645 hp Mercury VI, first took to the air from Eindhoven's Welschap airfield on 27 February 1936, flown by 43-year-old factory pilot Emil Meinecke. Bertus Somer, a young flying instructor and former fighter pilot, was subsequently engaged for spinning trials, but he panicked during an early test flight and nearly crashed the aircraft on 1 May, spreading word that the D.XXI was dangerous. To make matters worse, the NEIA had meanwhile decided to buy bombers rather than any fighters, and the metropolitan Dutch Army deemed the D.XXI too slow.

Former Messerschmitt test pilot 'Bubi' Knoetzsch had to be flown in to establish that spin recovery in the D.XXI was, in fact, normal, although the type was prone to stalling into a spin owing to its 'flat' wing, which had little dihedral and no washout. Famous French aerobatic pilot Michel Détroyat also went to Amsterdam to fly the D.XXI, and insisted that lateral stability should be increased.

Ilmavoimat (Finnish Air Force) Capt Gustaf 'Eka' Magnusson, who flew the prototype on 8 July 1936, did not share Détroyat's dim view, however, finding it a sharp, responsive fighter. The D.XXI's time-honoured mixed construction was also light yet strong, giving the aircraft good climbing and diving characteristics. As a result of Magnusson's recommendations, Fokker's seemingly ill-fated fighter emerged as the leading contender in Finland's 1936 fighter contest.

The Finns were already involved with Fokker designs, as in the spring of 1936 the company's C.X had been chosen to replace the earlier Fokker C.V army co-operation aircraft in *Ilmavoimat* service. This purchase was part of a new five-year plan, which also included a sufficient number of fighters to equip three squadrons with 27 aircraft each. The air force was standardising on the Mercury engine, and like the powerplant, the selected aircraft type was to be manufactured locally. This meant victory for the D.XXI over the competing PZL P.24, since Valtion Lentokonetehdas (VL), the Finnish State Aircraft Factory, could not cope with the Polish aeroplane's metal construction. Finland thus became the first customer for Fokker's new low-wing monoplane fighter, placing an order for seven aircraft on 18 November 1936, and also acquiring a licence to produce twice as many at the VL factory.

The prototype in its definitive form, with an enlarged rudder, a three-bladed propeller and the tailwheel fairing removed. Capt Van Lent took the aircraft aloft on its 151st flight (a dedicated aerial photography flight) on 18 June 1936. His Finnish colleague Eka Magnusson had flown it for the first time ten days earlier (*T Postma*)

During the first half of 1937 the government of Spain, where civil war had broken out the previous summer, secretly ordered 50 D.XXIs for local production, as well as G.I and C.X aircraft, and in July the Danish Army contracted for two D.XXIs, plus the rights to build ten more in its own workshops. Paradoxically, the type's conventional construction had made it a success. Finally, the Dutch government placed an order after all, signing a contract for 36 D.XXIs, as well as 36 twin-engined G.Is, in late 1937. The Dutch Army's change of mind came about because the D.XXI was considered suitable to fulfil a new 'frontal' fighter requirement. Production D.XXIs were to have 830 hp Mercury VII or VIII engines, although the Spaniards opted for the American Wright R-1820 Cyclone radial.

As it was owned by the NEIA, the single prototype was shipped to the colony in early 1937 – a move that inexplicably paralysed test and development flying until the first production aircraft for Finland flew in July 1937! This second D.XXI was briefly tested with a redesigned wing with much increased dihedral, as recommended by Détroyat, but nobody liked it and the original wing was restored without further doctoring. This aircraft alone was fitted with 20 mm Oerlikon cannon in underwing pods, replacing the two wing-mounted machine guns, at Finland's request.

Finnish D.XXIs were armed with two wing-mounted and two nose-mounted light machine guns as standard, and they had thicker undercarriage legs that were suitable for the fitting of skis rather than wheels so that the aircraft could remain operational during Finland's long snowy winters. The seven Dutch-built D.XXIs for Finland were shipped in November 1937, while the Danish pair were flown to Copenhagen in April 1938. The latter were provisionally fitted with the same undercarriage legs as seen on the Finnish examples, and older Mercury VI engines. Upon arriving in Denmark, one D.XII was fitted with indigenous Madsen cannon and tested at the Skallingen range, near Esbjerg. Impressed with the improvement in firepower, the Danes decided in July 1938 to go ahead with an armament of two 20 mm-calibre weapons plus two nose machine guns.

The top speed of the Finnish D.XXI was a disappointing 418 km/h (260 mph), and measures were taken to improve the performance of

This aircraft was only the second D XXI built, and the first production aircraft for Finland. Seen here at Schiphol, the airframe was exhibited at the Avia Fair in The Hague during August 1937, and ended up in an exhibition of Finnish war booty in Leningrad in 1940. It was also test flown with an increased-dihedral wing, and was the only D.XXI to see action with cannon armament (*T Postma*)

Dutch and Danish production aircraft, beyond the fitting of slim undercarriage legs. The airframe was cleaned up, a Hamilton rather than a Ratier three-bladed propeller was fitted and all four machine guns of the Dutch aircraft were installed in the wings, saving the weight of the synchronisation gear. The first Dutch Army D.XXI flew in May 1938. Official trials by the Netherlands Aviation Laboratory (NLL) yielded a 446 km/h (277 mph) top speed, or 460 km/h (286 mph) without armament, and NLL test pilot Henk van der Maas reported favourably on the fighter's handling.

Lacking a retractable undercarriage, armour plating, rubber self-sealing fuel tanks and other weight-increasing accessories to the extent that the engine was hand-cranked, the D.XXI boasted a rate-of-climb on a par with that of the Messerschmitt Bf 109E. Indeed, 5000 metres (16,400 ft) could be reached in just 6 min 36 sec. In September 1938 the Dutch altitude record was taken to 11,353 metres (37,248 ft) by a D.XXI flown by Fokker's new test pilot, Lt Hidde Leegstra.

Follow-on D.XXII designs, with bigger radial or inline engines, six guns and a retractable undercarriage, were never built, Fokker electing instead to concentrate on the unorthodox D.XXIII 'push-pull' fighter with twin engines in tandem. Minimum-change D.XXI variants with a retractable undercarriage and Bristol Perseus or Taurus engines also remained unbuilt. The last design work Fokker did on the D.XXI was a Pratt & Whitney R-1535 Twin Wasp Junior installation, requested by Finland in 1939 for further local D.XXI production, since Mercury engines were now earmarked for Bristol Blenheim bombers. The Wasp-powered D.XXI did not materialise until late 1940, by which time dramatic events in Europe had made the aircraft an exclusively Finnish affair.

The D.XXI was the last of a line of single-engined Fokker fighters, just 147 being produced in four countries – one prototype, 36 for the Netherlands, one in Spain, 12 for Denmark and 97 for Finland, the latter total including 55 Wasp-powered aircraft.

INTO SERVICE

Although the D.XXI never saw service in quantity in the Netherlands East Indies, the prototype was flown by the NEIA from April 1937. It is believed that it was eventually scrapped or destroyed by a Japanese attack in 1942.

Another lonely D.XXI was the sole example completed in Spain amid the chaos of the Spanish Civil War. The Hispano-Suiza plant in Guadalajara, which was to manufacture the D.XXI and C.X, had been evacuated to Alicante's La Rabasa Airport, and following a Nationalist air raid there the D.XXI production line was housed in a cleared convent by the anti-clerical Republican authorities. Soviet guns and M-100 engines were now to be fitted. Production of the C.X was moved to a village church. Only a production prototype of each type was completed, however. The D.XXI was reportedly test flown by Republican chief instructor pilot Mariano Palacios Palomar at Los Alcázares-El Carmoli airfield in October 1938, but the aircraft's fate is unknown and apparently no photographs survive. Hard evidence of the D.XXI programme exists, however, in the form of D.XXI undercarriage legs captured by the Nationalists and used on Hispano-Suiza HS-42 trainers.

FINNISH DEBUT

Carrying Finnish military serial numbers FR-76 to FR-82, and subsequently referred to as the 'I series', the seven Dutch-built aircraft for Finland were delivered to Amsterdam on 12 October 1937 and shipped north in crates, arriving within a month. These machines cost 1.1 million Finnish marks apiece without engines. The licence to manufacture the fighter was exploited on 7 June 1937 when an order for 14 aircraft was placed with VL. These 'II series' fighters, serialled FR-83 to FR-96, were completed between 11 November 1938 and 18 March 1939 at half the price of the Dutch-built examples. As early as 15 June 1937 an open licence was obtained from Fokker and a 'III series' of 21 aircraft put into production on the VL line. Completed between 16 March and 27 July

Photographed in the snow in front of hangar No 2 at Utti on 16 December 1937, FR-76 was the first D.XXI issued to LLv 24. Its unique 20 mm Oerlikon cannon armament was used successfully in the Winter War by 2Lt Olli Puhakka, who downed a DB-3M bomber with just 18 rounds fired from a distance of more than 500 metres (1640 ft) on 29 January 1940 (*Finnish Air Force*)

1939, just in time for the Winter War with the USSR, these fighters bore the serials FR-97 to FR-117.

The 'I series' D.XXIs were earmarked for *Lentolaivue* 24 (LLv 24) to replace the unit's ageing Gloster Gamecock biplanes. The first aircraft, FR-76, was received on 15 November 1937, and all but the last Dutch-built machine were in service with LLv 24 by the end of August 1938. Familiarisation was key, as the pilots had no previous experience of cantilever monoplane fighters, which were faster and possessed a much higher landing speed than their previous mounts.

After the 14 'II series' aircraft had been completed by VL they too were delivered to LLv 24 following flight-testing. The same pattern followed with the 'III series' fighters, although this time three D.XXIs went to LLv 12 for evaluation and the rest were supplied to LLv 26. The latter unit duly became the second squadron to receive the D.XXI, ten of them equipping two flights from 17 July 1939 onwards. However, by the time the Winter War commenced on 30 November that year, all D.XXIs had been transferred to LLv 24.

DUTCH DEPLOYMENT

The first D.XXIs for the Dutch Army's Aviation Branch (LVA) entered service with its single JaVA (*Jachtvliegtuigafdeling* – fighter squadron) at Schiphol in the summer of 1938. When the unit was put on alert during the Munich Crisis in late September it boasted one flight of the new monoplane fighters, one of D.XVIIs and one of C.Xs.

The D.XXI's initial operational usefulness was rather limited, however, as both Fokker and the army had still done little to make the aircraft a fully functional warplane. The Dutch version's tendency to lose its gun-bay covers was the least of its problems, this issue being solved by bolting them down. However, reloading the weapons now became a time-consuming task. The guns themselves often failed to cock in the air, froze at high altitude or jammed after manoeuvring – all straightforward issues that, nonetheless, were not all fixed until late 1939. Even proper alignment of the guns took ages.

The fighters, which lacked radio sets until early 1940, were also plagued by severe vibrations from the rotation of their main wheels in flight. Pilots

The first four D.XXIs for Dutch Army Aviation lined up at Schiphol on 29 August 1938. International tensions were on the rise, and this official photograph was clearly meant to impress, although the aircraft are still unarmed. The red, white and blue rudders were camouflaged from December 1938 (*T Postma*)

had to resort to applying their parking brakes in flight to eradicate the problem. To make matters worse, cracks and corrosion affected the Elektron light-alloy fuel tanks, and all Dutch D.XXIs were grounded during May–June 1939 while aluminium tanks were manufactured by Fokker. On a more positive note, all 36 aircraft, serialled 212 to 247, had been completed and flown by 1 March 1939.

Despite its intended 'frontal' air superiority role in support of the Dutch Field Army, the D.XXI served in an interim interceptor role from which it was never to be relieved. A batch of Curtiss CW-21B Interceptors was ordered only at the eleventh hour. Holland's air defences were mobilised on 7 April 1939 following Italy's annexation of Albania. Soon there were three small D.XXI units, namely the 1st JaVA at Schiphol, the 2nd JaVA at Rotterdam-Waalhaven and the 3rd JaVA at Soesterberg. The Army's expanding air arm changed its name from LVA to ML (Military Aviation) in 1939.

Wedged between England and northern Germany, Holland's airspace was frequently violated by belligerent air traffic from the very start of World War 2. German high-altitude reconnaissance aircraft had also begun photographing Dutch targets, since the strategic location of the country's ports and airfields meant that Holland was now on Hitler's 'to do' list. Whatever their nature, the incursions compromised the country's neutrality, and firm action was ordered against them, although initially without results.

Concerned, the Defence Minister paid a surprise early morning visit to Schiphol on 10 September. He found the 1st JaVA's readiness to be adequate, although some of the six D.XXIs shown to him with engines running were manned by mechanics and pilots still in pyjamas! That very day the squadron was deployed to Groningen-Eelde, near the north coast, where most of the intrusions were taking place.

The D.XXI's baptism of fire occurred three days later. That afternoon a German Heinkel He 115 seaplane shot down a Fokker T.VIIIW seaplane of the Dutch Navy, which somersaulted upon crash-landing near Ameland Island. The Heinkel landed to pick up the crew, but suffered damage when alighting, as did a German Dornier Do 18 flying boat of I/K.Fl.Gr 106, which arrived to render assistance. Eventually the He 115 was able to take off with the Dutch crew on board, but the Dornier was not so lucky. As it was trying to taxi out beyond Dutch territorial waters, three 1st JaVA D.XXIs arrived on the scene. The flight leader, Lt Frans Focquin de Grave, fired a burst across the Dornier's bow. The flying boat turned toward Ameland Island, but then turned round again as soon as the fighters appeared to be leaving. Focquin de Grave made a second pass, this time aiming at the Do 18 and wounding one of the crew. The latter abandoned the flying boat and paddled to the island to be

On 1 October 1939 flights were made to show the new orange triangle national insignia to the troops. The commander of the 1st JaVA, Capt Hein Schmidt Crans, took this photograph of Lt Herman Doppenberg in No 237 and *Wachtmeester* Willem Hateboer in No 241. On 10 May 1940 Doppenberg shot down a Bf 109 and Hateboer probably destroyed a Ju 52/3m (*T Postma*)

interned. The Do 18 was washed aground and slowly wrecked in the surf.

According to the Germans, the Fokker seaplane was shot down because the Dutch roundels too closely resembled the British or French national insignia. They were therefore hastily replaced by large orange triangle insignia and orange rudders as of 1 October. That month the 2nd JaVA moved to Eindhoven to guard the southeast of the country.

In the north, a 1st JaVA patrol failed to find an intruding reconnaissance aircraft on 26 October, but the Dornier Do 17 made a forced landing on the coast due to engine trouble and was inspected by personnel from the fighter squadron. On 2 November a Heinkel He 111 bomber was intercepted and fired at by 1st JaVA D.XXIs, but no hits were observed. On another occasion six D.XXIs led by the unit commander, Capt Hein Schmidt Crans, scrambled to intercept a large V formation which turned out to consist of a dozen geese! 'Hiccupping with laughter and sighing with relief, we flew back to our airfield at dusk', wrote Lt Henk van Overvest.

A general alert was called on 9 November, intelligence indicating signs of a German attack. The 1st JaVA moved to De Kooy naval airfield near Den Helder, as Eelde was too close to the German border. Nothing happened, however, Hitler having postponed his campaign in the West. The 1st JaVA returned to Eelde on 14 November, resuming neutrality enforcement. Five days later, in inclement weather, three pilots, led by Focquin de Grave, managed to intercept an intruder near Schiermonnikoog Island and attacked. Van Overvest recalled;

'It was a He 111 bomber, and its crew must have spotted us at almost the same time as we saw them, for the pilot immediately began climbing, overboosting his engines. I fired a burst abeam and then several from immediately aft, and the Heinkel's gunners replied, bullets hitting my tailplane and one hitting my engine, which, mercifully, kept running.'

Inspired by a soldiers' song, 'White Mice' markings were painted on the engine cowlings of the 1st JavA's D.XXIs (*T Postma*)

The 3rd JaVA flew both the D.XXI and the twin-engined Fokker G.I for a while. Although the much-celebrated G.I was a good aircraft, the G.I force used up a lot of resources that could have instead been allocated to the D.XXI force in order to triple it in size (*T Postma*)

Sgt Cor Sipkes, an experienced instructor pilot of the Air Defence Detachment, chased a German high-altitude reconnaissance aircraft on 23 November 1939. Upon returning to Soesterberg he forgot to release the parking wheel brakes, which were applied while in flight to prevent vibration, and somersaulted. Aircraft No 227 was repaired but not operational in May 1940, and it was captured by the Germans (*T Postma*)

The bomber reached German territory and force-landed on the German island of Borkum with a wounded gunner. 'At that time we didn't dislike the Germans enough to run mortal risks', van Overvest added. Nevertheless, his action is recognised by World War 2 air combat researcher Pieter Hooijmans as the first D.XXI 'kill'.

As this action confirmed, the 1st JaVA was arguably the top Dutch fighter squadron. The unit adopted its 'White Mice' insignia at around this time, the emblem being inspired by a soldier's song.

On 6 December a German Heinkel He 59 seaplane, which had alighted owing to fuel shortage, and several boats were reported in the shallow waters off Schiermonnikoog. An investigating flight of three D.XXIs, again led by Focquin de Grave, did not take action in this case, although the Dutch Navy was sending in a cruiser and three bombed-up Fokker T.VIIIWs just as the Germans managed to tow the seaplane into international waters. Focquin de Grave opened fire at an intruding Do 17 on the way back to Eelde.

Trainee D.XXI pilots of the Air Defence Detachment at Soesterberg. All of these men were to fly the type during the May war. *Wachtmeester* Jaap van Zuijlen, in the centre, was killed while attacking a He 111. Lt Hans Plesman, second, and Sgt Ben De Geus, on the right, shared in the destruction of a Ju 52/3m on 10 May and saw a lot of action throughout the five-day battle. Lt Bik, on the left, emerged from hospital to lead the first escort flight to Rotterdam on 11 May. Sgt Burger, fourth, was the only D.XXI pilot to return from the second escort flight. Aircraft No 233 was flown by Sgt Slag of the 'White Mice' 1st JaVA on the morning of 10 May, and it was later damaged on the ground (*via F Gerdessen*)

In early December the new Fighter Group Field Army used its first D.XXIs to raise its own 1st JaVA at Soesterberg, which we will call the Field Army 1st JaVA to distinguish it from the 'White Mice' 1st JaVA. The 3rd JaVA, which was in the process of receiving Fokker G.Is, had moved to Rotterdam-Waalhaven during the November alert, leaving its D.XXIs with an Air Defence Detachment at Soesterberg to cover the central part of the country. The Detachment doubled as a D.XXI operational conversion unit, and on 22 November one of its trainee pilots was killed when his aircraft crashed in thick fog. The next day Sgt Sipkes, one of the instructors, somersaulted while landing at Soesterberg, having forgotten to release the parking brakes after chasing a German high-altitude reconnaissance aircraft.

On 17 December five D.XXIs of the Detachment, along with two G.Is from the 4th JaVA, scrambled to intercept another reconnaissance aircraft, but could not get close. Watching the scene from the ground, the Detachment commander, Lt Frans van Breemen, saw a fresh intruder coming in from the east, high in a clear sky. He took off in his last D.XXI and eventually managed to get within range, but his guns jammed after a short burst. Van Breemen, an airline captain in peacetime, had to content himself with noting down the identity letters of the pressurised He 111 of Oberst Rowehl's special reconnaissance unit.

Six days into 1940, Detachment pilot Lt Thate dived on an unidentified aircraft and collided with it. Unfortunately his adversary was a 4th JaVA G.I, which crashed after the crew bailed out. Thate was able to land his D.XXI with only a bent undercarriage leg. The Air Defence Detachment was disbanded in late February, the Field Army 1st JaVA being given the air defence role instead.

In the south, the 2nd JaVA failed to catch any intruders, although two D.XXI pilots became offenders themselves when they entered German airspace owing to a navigational error. In February the 1st and 2nd JaVAs changed places, allowing the latter squadron to build experience in the busier north. On the 20th, 2nd JaVA pilots chased a He 111 that zigzagged towards the border at treetop height and managed to escape.

Lt Govert Steen in his Austin sports car at Soesterberg in the spring of 1940. The D.XXI is No 215, which he ended up landing on Kijkduin beach on 10 May. Steen hijacked a Luftwaffe Fokker T.VIIIW seaplane to escape to England in May 1941, and was killed in a Spitfire of No 129 Sqn near Le Havre on 5 June 1942 (*T Postma*)

WINTER WAR

The Ribbentrop-Molotov Pact between Germany and the Soviet Union, signed on 23 August 1939, ensured non-aggression between the two nations. Secret protocols in the treaty defined the territorial spheres of influence both countries would have over Poland following its subsequent invasion, and left the Baltic countries and Finland in the Soviet Union's sphere of interest.

Germany launched a thoroughly prepared attack on Poland on 1 September 1939, and it had seized the western parts of the country in just three weeks. According to the Pact, the Soviet Union occupied the eastern provinces of Poland. At the same time the Soviets demanded air and naval bases from then independent Estonia, Latvia and Lithuania and, thanks to weak resistance, got them.

At first the Soviets tried to diplomatically acquire military bases in Finland too, thus shifting the border further west away from Leningrad. In return Finland would get twice the area of wilderness further north in Soviet Karelia. Everything was disguised under the pretext of improving the safety of Leningrad, which the Finns duly suspected was a ruse. As a sovereign country, Finland responded with a firm refusal. The Soviet Union duly abandoned the non-aggression pact and attacked Finland on 30 November 1939, starting the Winter War – truly a struggle between David and Goliath.

During the autumn of 1939 the Red Army had concentrated troops on the Karelian Isthmus (7th Army) and at Aunus-Porajärvi (8th Army), Repola-Uhtua-Kantalahti (9th Army) and Petsamo (14th Army). This meant that on the eve of the Winter War, 450,000 men in more than 20 divisions, supported by 2000 artillery pieces, 2000 armoured vehicles and 2318 aircraft, were lined up along the 1600 km-long (1000-mile) Russo-Finnish border.

The aircraft assigned to the VVS (*Voyenno-Vozdushnye Sily* – Soviet Military Air Force) on the Finnish front were split up as follows;

Aircraft	7th Army	8th Army	9th Army	14th Army	Baltic Fleet	Total
SB	536	20	-	24	51	631
DB-3/3M	149	-	-	22	53	224
I-16	359	33	-	18	129	539
I-153	102	-	-	17	22	141
I-15	204	42	15	15	88	364
Others	283	-	-	-	136	419
Total	**1633**	**95**	**15**	**96**	**479**	**2318**

This huge air armada would fly an average of 1000 sorties per day. By comparison, on the main front of the Karelian Isthmus (7th Army sector) the Finns could muster five divisions, 300 pieces of artillery, 20 tanks and just 114 serviceable aircraft.

FIGHTER COMMAND

The reorganisation of the *Ilmavoimat* on 1 January 1938 transformed its air stations into flexible aviation regiments. *Lentoasema* 1 at Utti became *Lentorykmentti* (LeR) 2, which had at its disposal LLvs 24 and 26 – the first fighter regiment in Finland came in to existence.

During the course of 1938 and the first half of 1939 LLv 24 handed over its obsolete Gamecocks to training units, and all three flights became fully equipped with D.XXIs. In addition, LLv 26 received sufficient Fokker fighters to equip two flights, which operated alongside the unit's ageing Bristol Bulldog IVA biplanes.

The Finnish fighter defences were all concentrated into LeR 2, commanded by Lt Col Richard Lorentz. He had two fighter squadrons, which he had moved away from Utti during the mobilisation of November 1939. The D.XXIs of LLv 26 were subsequently transferred to LLv 24 on 26 November 1939, being used primarily to equip the 1st and 5th Flights. The order of battle for LeR 2 on 30 November 1939 was as follows;

LeR 2
Regimental Commander, Lt Col Richard Lorentz, with HQ at Immola

LLv 24
Commander, Capt Gustaf Magnusson, with HQ at Immola
– 1st Flight, Capt Eino Carlsson at Immola with six D.XXIs
– 2nd Flight, 1Lt Jaakko Vuorela at Suur-Merijoki with six D.XXIs
– 3rd Flight, 1Lt Eino Luukkanen at Immola with six D.XXIs
– 4th Flight, Capt Gustaf Magnusson at Immola with seven D.XXIs
– 5th Flight, 1Lt Leo Ahola at Immola with ten D.XXIs

LLv 26
Commander, Capt Erkki Heinilä, with HQ at Heinjoki
– Det Heinilä, Capt Erkki Heinilä at Heinjoki with ten Bulldog IVAs

The *Ilmavoimat's* modern fighter force consisted exclusively of LLv 24 and its 35 D.XXIs. Its CO, Capt 'Eka' Magnusson, would show exceptional tactical and personal leadership during the Winter War. The Fokker fighters, split into five flights that were ready to be deployed around southeastern Finland in response to Soviet offensives, were manned by well trained and well motivated pilots committed to defending their country. LLv 24's task was to protect the traffic junctions in southeastern Finland and prevent Soviet attacks on and through the Finnish-controlled Karelian Isthmus – a strategically important land 'bridge' up to 110 km (69 miles) in width between Lake Ladoga and the Gulf of Finland. Magnusson also gave strict orders to his pilots to avoid fighter duels. The D.XXI was not manoeuvrable enough to 'mix it' with Soviet Polikarpov fighters, but it was perfectly suited to the role of interceptor. Even if it lacked speed, the Fokker had a good rate of climb and could always pull away from its foes in a dive.

FIGHTER TACTICS

As early as 1934 then Maj Lorentz had discovered while commanding LLv 24, flying Gloster Gamecocks, that contrary to the traditional fighter formation of a lead aircraft and two wingmen, a pair of fighters was much more flexible and better suited to most tactical conditions. And their number could easily be increased to a four-aircraft *swarm* if required.

Before assuming command of LLv 24, Maj Magnusson had paid a number of visits to other air forces, including spending three months with the Luftwaffe fighter unit JG 132 *Richthofen*. The Germans had

also abandoned the three-aircraft basic formation in favour of the 'finger-four'. Briefings from Magnusson duly convinced the leadership of the *Ilmavoimat* that the basic two-aircraft formation, and tactics associated with it, were sound.

Owing to a lack of funds in the prewar *Ilmavoimat*, the training of would-be fighter pilots was not as thorough as it could have been. The elementary phase of the curriculum was adequately taught, but advanced training did not embrace all possible modes of offence. This was primarily because it had been decided that two types of attack against bombers, or three at the most, were enough. These three methods, and the associated gunnery skills needed to carry them out, were thoroughly rehearsed by students. The teaching of anti-bomber tactics served both the doctrine and economical limits of the *Ilmavoimat* at that time too. It was also assumed that in a conflict bomber formations would arrive without a fighter escort, which indeed they did during the first half of the war.

The machine guns fitted in the D.XXI were usually aligned to converge at 150 metres (160 yd), but the pilots were trained to refrain from firing until just 50 metres (55 yd) from their target. Getting so close was somewhat risky, but at that distance behind the bomber the attacker had two major advantages – he was within the minimum firing distance for the bomber's defensive weapons, and he could not miss. Moreover, rifle-calibre machine gun fire did not cause the bomber to explode.

The Winter War would show that the basic fighting pair formation, with its multiples of two, was correct. This gave a tactical advantage to the Finns, who would remain on the offensive at all times even when faced with a numerically superior enemy. This doctrine remained at the heart of the *Ilmavoimat* throughout World War 2.

REPELLING BOMBERS

On 30 November 1939, the first day of the Winter War, 200 aircraft of the Soviet air forces bombed many towns and airfields in southern Finland, while communist fighters patrolled unmolested midway along the Karelian Isthmus. The pilots of LeR 2 failed to intercept the invaders owing to poor weather.

The Finnish capital, Helsinki, was among the bombed locations, with ordnance from eight DB-3s of 1st MTAP KBF (*Minno-Torpednyy-Aviatsionnyy Polk Krasnoznamyonnyy Baltiyskiy Flot* – Mine-torpedo Aviation Regiment of the Red Banner Baltic Fleet) killing close to 100

Camouflaged FR-86 of 2/LLv 24 at Utti on 1 December 1939. On this day the flight leader, 1Lt Jaakko Vuorela, scored the squadron's first aerial victory when he claimed an SB bomber shot down (*SA-kuva*)

SSgt Lauri Nissinen leans on the right undercarriage leg of his D.XXI in late 1939. A member of the 5th Flight, he was one of 12 Winter War D.XXI aces to claim five or more victories. Nissinen's final score reached 32.5 kills, and he became a recipient of the Mannerheim Cross on 5 July 1942 (*J Dahl*)

civilians and wounding another 200. The attack on Helsinki in particular resonated with foreign nations appalled by the naked aggression of the USSR, and resulted in the Finns receiving military aid from France, Britain and Italy. Ironically, recent research in the Russian archives has revealed that the bombing of downtown Helsinki was a mistake, the DB-3s' actual target being the oil storages and harbour at Herttoniemi, several kilometres further east.

The next day 250 unescorted bombers were in the air, attacking many of the same targets they had hit 24 hours earlier. In response, the D.XXIs took off in pairs, led by Capt Magnusson. This time unaffected by poor weather, the pilots of LLv 24 completed 59 sorties and claimed 11 bombers destroyed in the Viipuri-Lappeenranta area – eight SBs from 41st SBAP (*Skorostnoy Bombardirovohchnyy Aviatsionnyy Polk* – High-Speed Bomber Aviation Regiment) and three SBs from 24th SBAP.

The first fell at 1205 hrs to the guns of the 2nd Flight leader, 1Lt Jaakko Vuorela, and the last at 1440 hrs to the leader of the 5th Flight, 1Lt Leo Ahola. Vuorela also claimed a second SB, while the other successful pilots were Capt Gustaf Magnusson, 1Lts Eino Luukkanen and Jussi Räty, 2Lt Pekka Kokko and Sgts Lasse Heikinaro, Lauri Nissinen, Lauri Rautakorpi and Kelpo Virta. No combat reports exist for these first encounters as no such forms were made available to LLv 24 until some three weeks later. However, Magnusson insisted that every pilot who engaged the enemy should write down his experiences. His own personal account reads as follows;

'1/12/39 at 1410-1445 hrs. Based on an announcement that a Soviet bomber formation was approaching Imatra, we took off. We met the formation above Imatra. I attacked the bomber flying on the extreme right wing, shooting first along its fuselage. When the firing did not seem to have any effect, I aimed my fire at its starboard engine, which started to smoke after a few bursts.

'I had to interrupt my attack since the bomber to the left of my target had reduced speed. It was now about 70 metres [75 yd] off my port side, with its dorsal gunner firing all the time at me. I slowed down behind this second aeroplane and sent it down in flames. The aircraft crashed, burning into the ground.

'Since the squadron only had normal bullets and tracers, it was not possible to gain results with a small amount of ammunition. I fired 1200 rounds from my machine, FR-99.'

Magnusson's obvious skill, and determination, during the course of this mission was a clear example to his men of what was expected of

LLv 24 CO Gustaf Erik 'Eka' Magnusson was promoted to the rank of major on 6 December 1939, and he is seen here giving a speech at Immola on this occasion. Behind him are FR-105 and FR-106 (*I Juutilainen*)

them. Indeed, the CO's achievements in the unit's first encounter with the enemy proved that the tactics adopted by LLv 24 prewar would indeed be effective in combat.

Although the unit had tasted tremendous success on 1 December, this was tempered by its first fatality. Tragically, Sgt Matti Kukkonen was shot down in error in FR-77 by Finnish anti-aircraft guns at Viipuri. A further materiel loss occurred when the squadron's hack de Havilland DH 60 Moth MO-111 was hit by a bomb at Immola and burned out.

On 18 December 1939 'friendly' flak hit the fuel tank of FR-104, flown by 3/LLv 24 leader 1Lt Eino Luukkanen. He made a forced landing in a frozen field at Kavantsaari, but nosed over (*Finnish Aviation Museum*)

From 2 December further poor weather kept the D.XXIs on the ground for almost three weeks. Conditions finally improved sufficiently enough on 18 December to allow LLv 24 to complete 30 sorties, but most of the D.XXIs could not engage the enemy bombers owing to persistent poor weather on the Karelian Isthmus. Nevertheless, 1Lt Jorma Karhunen and his wingman encountered a squadron of SBs, and Karhunen managed to hit one of them. Although he claimed to have damaged the fast bomber, post-war research revealed that the aeroplane, belonging to 24th SBAP, failed to make it back to base.

The persistent poor weather and associated heavy snowfall ended on 19 December, allowing Soviet air power to target the strategically important fort of Saarenpää – it suffered an estimated 500 bomb hits. Consequently LLv 24 flew 58 sorties over the Karelian Isthmus in an attempt to defend the fort, and was engaged in combat on 22 occasions between 1050 hrs and 1520 hrs. The Soviets lost seven SBs, six from 44th SBAP and five DB-3s from other regiments.

SSgt Kelpo Virta was the first to see action that day, although his claims were for two I-16 fighters from 25th IAP (*Istrebitel'naya Aviatsionnaya Polk* – fighter aviation regiment) destroyed. Ground troops observed the crashes of both Polikarpovs, giving Virta full credit for his successes.

LLv 24's squadron adjutant interviewed every pilot engaged in aerial combat on 19 December and compiled a summary in which the events

Seen here at Siikakangas in June 1940, FR-92 belonged to LLv 32. It still sports the tactical marking 'Black 5' favoured by 1Lt 'Pelle' Sovelius, 4/LLv 24's deputy leader in the Winter War. He had claimed seven and three shared victories all while flying this aeroplane (*Finnish Air Force Museum*)

were recorded in the style of an official combat report. 1Lt Per Sovelius, who flew FR-92, recalled;

'On 19/12/39 from 0955 hrs to 1105 hrs on air combat patrol, I was leading the third pair, with Sgt Ikonen on my wing. We took off upon being alerted. I was flying over Antrea when a radio call informed us of enemy aircraft to the southwest. Somewhere near Kämärä I observed a seven-aeroplane SB formation and started the chase. The SBs initially flew in a southwesterly direction before turning south. We did not gain on them. We did, however, observe a further three SBs off to the side of the main formation, and although they were flying roughly in the same direction, they were closer to us.

'Sgt Ikonen got in behind the SB on the starboard side of the three-aeroplane formation and shot at it from very close range until the bomber burst into flames at an altitude of 2000 metres [6500 ft] over Kipinola. I tried to get behind the port SB, but did not have enough speed. I observed another three SBs heading southwest and went after them, but they too were too fast for me to catch. These aeroplanes were throwing out leaflets.

'During the chase I observed another three SBs a little below me, heading southwards. These aircraft were much closer, and I picked the port bomber as my target and shot first into its rear fuselage, which caused the dorsal gunner to cease firing. After this I aimed at the port engine, which began to smoke and finally caught fire. The aeroplane fell away to starboard and dived towards the sea close to Seivästö, about ten kilometres [six miles] from the coast. I then fired at the starboard SB, whereupon its right engine started to pour smoke, but it remained in formation with the lead aeroplane.

'Breaking off my attack, I headed for home at an altitude of 3000 metres [9800 ft]. When I was about five kilometres [three miles] from land I observed anti-aircraft artillery explosions. As I flew over the southern coastline of Lake Muolaanjärvi two I-16s managed to take me by surprise, attacking from out of the sun. I came to my senses when bullets rattled into my aircraft. I pulled instantly towards them, but soon realised that the I-16 was more manoeuvrable than the Fokker. I tried to tighten my turns, but only once got the enemy in my sight, and fired a short burst. It was then that I noticed that I only had ammunition remaining in one gun. Once, while trying to turn as tight as possible, I lost control of my D.XXI and slipped into a spin. I continued to take all sorts of evasive action, and once down at low level I managed to shake off my pursuers. By then I was near Heinjoki.

'Both I-16s had attacked simultaneously, and obviously to avoid a collision they did not get in directly behind me. This forced them to shoot with a small deflection. Judging by the amount of tracer in the air, the I-16 pilots seemed to fire all the time, even when my aeroplane was clearly out of their sights.

'After the mission my aircraft was found to have taken two hits – one round had struck the tailplane and the other had gone in through the machine gun compression bottle hatch and out through the underside of the fuselage.'

On 20 December LLv 24 added two fighters and one bomber to its score over the Karelian Isthmus. Making the most of benign weather conditions the following morning, the Soviets sent 300 bombers to attack targets in southeastern Finland. LLv 24 responded by flying 62 interception

1Lt Per Sovelius, the deputy leader of 4/LLv 24, is all harnessed-up in front of his aircraft, FR-92. He was the second-highest-scoring D.XXI ace of the Winter War, with 7.5 aerial victories all gained in this aircraft (*Finnish Aviation Museum*)

sorties, during the course of which three DB-3s were shot down over the Karelian Isthmus.

Bad luck in the form of D.XXIs from LLv 24 hit 44th SBAP again on 23 December when at around 1100 hrs six SBs were downed on the Karelian Isthmus, 1Lt Sarvanto claiming two. Magnusson, who was flying FR-99, described his shooting down of one bomber;

'Sgt Kinnunen, flying off my left flank, observed nine SBs above Vuoksenranta. I dived after Sgt Kinnunen, who broke off his attack on the bombers after thinking that I was a pursuing I-16. I continued after the formation and caught it over Kiviniemi. I chose the rearmost bomber on the left flank as my target. First, I aimed at the starboard engine, which started to smoke. Thereafter, I shot at the port engine until it too burst into flames, whereupon the aeroplane began to descend.

'Tactically, the enemy crews worked well, lowering their undercarriages simultaneously to reduce speed, while the pilot flying the aircraft next to the one I was attacking reduced speed so that his rear gunner had a better position from which to fire at me.

'The aircraft I had attacked hit the ground at Lempaalanjärvi at noon.'

The day's engagements totalled 21, and during fighter duels a further two I-16s from 7th IAP and two from 64th IAP were shot down. Sgt Pentti Tilli accounted for both of the former, with 1Lt Urho Nieminen and 2Lt Heikki Ilveskorpi downing the latter machines. One D.XXI suffered damage from enemy fire in return and Sgt Tauno Kaarma was injured when he crashed FR-111.

By 25 December Finnish ground forces had stopped all the advances of the Soviet armies along the 1000-mile-long border, ushering in a five-week stalemate. The extremely cold winter weather, with temperatures routinely below -30ºC and below -40ºC on several days, did not favour the attacking Russians.

25 December also saw the D.XXIs of LLv 24 destroy two SB bombers of 6th DBAP (*Dal'nebombardirovochnyy Aviatsionnyy Polk* – Long-range Bomber Aviation Regiment) over the Karelian Isthmus. That same day, further north, the 3rd Flight found itself in the thick of the action as well. It had recently been strengthened in number to become Detachment Luukkanen, prior to its transfer to Värtsilä in support of troops defending the northern coast of Lake Ladoga. On the 25th its pilots brought down four SBs of 18th BAP, 1Lt Jorma Karhunen and Sgt Toivo Vuorimaa claiming two apiece. Two days later, over the Karelian Isthmus, the Soviets lost three SBs of 2nd SBAP, while WO Viktor Pyötsiä shot

An ace who claimed all of his kills in the Winter War, 2Lt Toivo Vuorimaa of 1/LLv 24 was assigned aircraft FR-93, in which he downed four aircraft. He served an instructor during the Continuation War (*J Sarvanto*)

The personnel of Detachment Luukkanen at Värtsilä come together for a group photograph on Christmas Eve 1939. They are, from left to right, unknown assistant mechanic, unknown armourer, mechanic P Hannula, mechanic J Paajanen, Sgt Ilmari Juutilainen, assistant mechanic T Karhu, SSgt Pentti Tilli, mechanic P Heino, 1Lt Tatu Huhanantti, mechanic V Eve, Detachment L CO 1Lt Eino Luukkanen, mechanic U Raunio, 1Lt Jorma Karhunen, assistant mechanic K Pyötsiä and mechanic E Horppu (*E Luukkanen*)

Flying FR-106 with 3/LLv 24 in the Winter War, top-scoring Finnish fighter ace WO Ilmari Juutilainen claimed two aerial victories. He subsequently flew the Brewster and Bf 109G, and was finally credited with 94 kills. Juutilainen was twice awarded the Mannerheim Cross, on 24 April 1942 and 28 June 1944 (*Finnish Air Force Museum*)

down two I-15bis fighters north of Lake Ladoga.

On 31 December Sgt Ilmari Juutilainen, who was a member of LLv 24's Detachment Luukkanen and the future top scoring Finnish ace with 94 kills, shot a lone I-16 off 1Lt Karhunen's tail over the northern shore of Lake Ladoga.

LLv 24 had steadily built its tally of aerial victories to 54, despite persistent poor weather, during its first month of operations. In that time it had lost just a solitary D.XXI (to friendly fire), with a second fighter damaged. However, the small number of D.XXIs in Finland meant that LLv 24 had had to focus on intercepting Soviet bombers over the Karelian Isthmus, rather than the almost daily air raids on southern Finland, where aircraft attacked numerous targets with impunity.

The first month of the war had gone well for the Finns, much to their surprise. On the Karelian Isthmus the Red Army advance had been stopped along the main defensive line. Between Lake Ladoga and the Arctic Sea Soviet troops had been halted in spite of initial difficulties. Furthermore, north of Lake Ladoga, the Finns had started to regain lost territory. At Suomussalmi, various battles had ended in a brilliant victory for the Finnish army, while at Salla all Soviet advances had been stopped. The Red Army's bombardment of Finnish cities and towns had also proven to be less effective than previously feared. Finally, the campaign waged by the Red Banner Baltic Fleet on Finland's left flank had been ineffective at best.

In the wake of these failures, the Soviet supreme command called a halt to its offensive operations and ordered 7th and 13th Armies to mass on the Karelian Isthmus where it formed part of the Northwestern Front.

On 1 January 4/LLv 24 had been sent to Utti after it had been discovered that Soviet bombers were using the Finnish railway network for orientation when en route to industrial targets further inland.

That same day, north of Lake Ladoga, D.XXIs claimed two bombers as the unit's first victories of 1940.

Soviet aircraft were conspicuous by their absence until the 5th, when LLv 24 carried out 35 interceptions and claimed three bombers shot down over the Karelian Isthmus.

During the morning of 6 January 17 DB-3Ms of 6th DBAP took off in two formations from Estonia to bomb the ammunition factory complex at Kuopio, in eastern Finland. The first nine aeroplanes bombed as planned, but the second group of eight bombers drifted too

Pilots of LLv 24 at Joutseno on New Year's Day 1940. In the back row, from left to right, are WO Yrjö Turkka, Sgt Lasse Heikinaro, 1Lt Jorma Sarvanto and Danish Volunteer 1Lt Erhard Frijs. In the front row, again from left to right, are Sgts Risto Heiramo, Eero Kinnunen and Tauno Kaarma. Behind them is FR-81/'Black 7' (*J Sarvanto*)

far west and crossed the Gulf of Finland south of Utti, where 4/LLv 24 was then based. In the air that morning was 1Lt 'Pelle' Sovelius, who caught the bombers at 1010 hrs at 3000 metres (10,000 ft) and shot down the aircraft on the extreme left-hand side of the formation. The remaining seven DB-3Ms followed the railway line to Kuopio, released their bombs without causing any serious damage and returned by the same route. Meanwhile, 1Lt Sarvanto had taken off, and he met the returning bombers. His report on what happened next read as follows;

'The 4th Flight, consisting of six Fokker aeroplanes, was temporarily posted to Utti on 1 January and tasked with intercepting bomber missions heading to inner parts of Finland via the important railway junction at Kouvola. The Flight was led by Maj G Magnusson, the commander of LLv 24. The weather was usually cloudy and no enemy aeroplanes were found during the handful of patrols we flew on 4 and 5 January.

'On the 6th the weather for enemy bombing raids was quite favourable. A layer of cloud hung at 300-400 metres [1000-1300 ft], with gaps here and there, and above it was a strange dim layer, which extended up to an altitude of 4000-5000 metres [13,000-16,000 ft]. The horizontal visibility was rather limited due to this dim layer.

'I was leading the second pair of D.XXIs in FR-97, my wingman being reservist 2Lt O Mustonen. We performed a couple of half-hour search missions in the morning, but found no enemy. However, 1Lt P Sovelius, who was flying from Lappeenranta to Utti, heard radio messages sent to us about enemy bombers and, using them, found eight Soviet machines at an altitude of 3000 metres [10,000 ft] heading north. He attacked from the rear and fired at two of the outermost aircraft, one of which crashed and burned out on the ground.

'After 1040 hrs, having received no more reports of enemy aircraft, we returned to Utti and had our breakfast in peace in the back of the hangar while the aeroplanes were covered with sheets out in the open. 2Lt Mustonen and I had been given the job of being the first responders should the bombers return. The second patrol was to be led by Lt Sovelius and the third by Maj Magnusson.

'While eating breakfast it occurred to me that perhaps the aircraft engaged by Sovelius would return via the same route, and therefore we

Pilots of 4/LLv 24 at Joutseno in January 1940. They are, from left to right, Sgt Martti Alho, 1Lt Frits Rasmussen, 2Lt Tapani Harmaja and 1Lt Per Sovelius. Behind them is Maj Magnusson's mount, FR-99 (*J Sarvanto*)

The first Finnish fighter ace, 1Lt Jorma Sarvanto, sitting in his aircraft, FR-97/'White 2', at Utti on 6 January 1940. On this particular day, as a member of the 4th Flight, he downed six DB-3M bombers in just four minutes south of Utti. 'Zamba' Sarvanto was the top-scoring fighter pilot of the Winter War with 13 confirmed victories (*J Sarvanto*)

should take off immediately and be ready for them when they appeared. Having proposed this to the others, I then got up in the middle of the meal and ordered the mechanics to start the engines of the two D.XXIs in my patrol. I also fastened my parachute.

'A few minutes later a message came through by telephone that seven bombers had been spotted heading south over Mikkeli level, if I remember correctly. I shouted, "Second pair to their aeroplanes", before running to my aircraft. Having quickly climbed into the cockpit, I simultaneously switched on the radio and started the engine, which the mechanics had not yet done. The radio messages were precise enough for me to follow the bombers' route on my map grid square by grid square. I saw that the bombers were heading straight for Utti. I also took into account the delay in transmitting the messages, knowing from experience that the bombers were already in the next air-surveillance grid square, rather that the one relayed to me.

'We received the order to scramble over the radio. At that point my wingman's mechanic ran over to my cockpit and told me that they could not start Mustonen's aeroplane. Upon hearing this news I waved him away and I pushed open the throttle, taxiing from the dispersal area across the airfield and then taking off to the north. I configured my aeroplane so that it would climb at the optimum angle, its speed at this point being about 170 km/h [105 mph].

'The weather had improved since my morning patrol, the lower cloud layer having gone and the sun now beginning to shine. There was plenty of haze, however.

'During the climb I listened to the radio, and the messages I received were very clear. Only transmissions relating to the seven bombers were sent, and they told me that the aircraft were still heading towards me. I occasionally glimpsed behind me and saw that I was alone.

'Eventually I saw the light-coloured bellies of the bombers, which remained in formation. Their blue undersides blended in pretty well with the blue of the sky, so if I had been further away from them they may have passed me by without being noticed. I was a few hundred metres below the bombers, and I turned to the south to make sure that they remained behind me. Continuing to climb, I kept my eyes on the enemy. They flew over me with a considerable speed advantage, and for a moment I was in the firing sector of their nose gunners – I was only 200-300 metres [220-330 yd] away, but I did not observe any rounds being fired in my direction. I continued to climb, but not so steeply now, until I was about 600 metres [650 yd] behind the formation. I was now at their altitude.

'My throttle was still fully open, as it had been since I had taken off. The altimeter showed 2000 metres [6500 ft] and my watch said exactly 1200 hrs. I decreased the fuel mixture in order to get full power from my engine, and, judging by the sound of it, it was certainly running at full revolutions. I turned off the radio, not wishing to be bothered by any messages, which now seemed unnecessary. I also took occasional glimpses behind me so as not to be taken by surprise by other enemy aircraft. I checked all armament systems, including the gun compression bottle gauge, and opened the cover for the Goertz gunsight.

'Now in level flight, I had gradually caught up with the seven bombers flying ahead of me. With the aid of the gunsight, I estimated their range as 500 metres [540 yd]. The bombers were flying almost line abreast, being only an aeroplane's span apart. On the left was a very slightly rearwards-staggered echelon, while those to the right were in a line. There was no evident stagger in height.

'I approached the aeroplanes so that I was in a blind spot created by the rudders of the two leftmost bombers. At this point the aircraft third from the left appeared to me to be in the most dangerous position. I had hoped that the Soviet gunners would be feeling carefree after a long bombing mission, but at a range of about 300 metres [330 yd] my aeroplane rattled unpleasantly and tracers bounced all around. Up to now I had flown straight ahead, but now I swung my aircraft from side to side so as to make it harder for the gunners to aim. I was still approaching at a good speed, and my gunsight was filled with the aeroplane on the extreme left. The range was down to about 200 metres [220 yd] when I fired my first short burst, which appeared to hit.

'I then immediately turned my attention to the third aircraft from the left. My short burst silenced the rear gunner, and I then knocked out his comrade in the aeroplane that was second from the left. Now I was only 100 metres [110 yd] from the leftmost bomber, which was trailing light smoke from my previous attack. I fired two short bursts into the smoking engine, which caught fire, and then at very close range I fired a short burst into the third aeroplane, which also burst into flames.

'Russian bomber crews had recently adopted an interesting defensive tactic. When a fighter was harassing one side of a formation, one or two bombers from the other side of the formation would slow down undetected and move in behind the fighter, giving their nose gunners an excellent opportunity to return fire. So as to avoid this happening to me, I swung to the right side of the formation and kept firing short bursts, first at the most dangerous rear gunners and then, as was my practice, at the starboard engines.

'All of a sudden the aeroplane on the extreme right pulled up to starboard and flew out of the formation, smoking heavily. I left it behind and continued to work over the remaining aircraft. When I took a glimpse to the right I observed that the bomber that had just broken away from the formation was now fully ablaze and going down in a spiral dive.

'Throughout the engagement I used only short bursts, and never fired unless I was sure of hitting the target. Striking the bombers was not particularly difficult, as the firing distance was mostly under 50 metres [55 yd], and occasionally just the length of the DB-3M. I remember missing only once, when the enemy pilot pulled his aeroplane sharply up when I opened fire.

'I had the red sun of January shining on my face through the layer of haze during the action, except when columns of black smoke from burning aeroplanes cast a shadow. Initially, the enemy pilots had ignored the advantage of the sun, since at first they flew in a southeasterly direction. However, upon seeing me, they took a southerly course directly at the sun.

'My sixth victim was the most difficult to despatch. As with the other bombers, I had already knocked out the rear turret of the seventh aircraft before turning my attention back to the sixth aircraft. Firing from close range, I used relatively long bursts from the synchronised fuselage guns only, as the ammunition for the faster-firing unsynchronised wing guns was already exhausted. After the sixth aeroplane finally caught fire, I moved closer to the remaining one and aimed at the starboard engine from above and behind. I pulled the trigger but the guns were quiet, despite me cocking them again and again. I had run out of ammunition, so all I could do was break off my attack and return home.

'I made a shallow dive and began to fly at low revolutions towards Utti, examining my aeroplane. Although I could see no signs of damage, the engine was shaking and the starboard wing and aileron resembled a Swiss cheese. The time was 1210 hrs.

'During the return flight I looked at the scenery. Black columns of smoke rose vertically into the air, and here and there burning aeroplanes could be seen on the ground. I tried to remember their locations.

'While preparing to land I tried to pump the flaps down, but the pump did not work, having been shot out. I now had to land at a greater speed than usual. Unfortunately another landing Fokker disturbed me at the point of touchdown, but I did not want to go round again because I was not sure that my riddled aeroplane would stand it. I landed across the airfield and fortunately the deep and soft snow killed my speed.

'After taxiing in to the hangar the mechanics started cheering, as they had seen most of the combat from the base. When I told them there were six bombers in all, I was tossed into the air several times. Because of the damage to my machine I could not make any further flights that day, so I sat by the phone while others awaited the order to scramble, mostly sitting in their aircraft.

'I later saw the exact locations of the crashes on a map from the Kouvola air surveillance area centre. The first two were side-by-side on the edge of

'Zamba' Sarvanto shows off the rudder fabric of one of the DB-3M bombers from 6th DBAP that he shot down on 6 January 1940. This photograph was taken during a press conference held at the Immola officers' club two days after Sarvanto's memorable mission (*SA-kuva*)

the Haukkasuo swamp, south of Utti, then two almost in line and finally two again close by Tavastila. The distance between the two aircraft furthest apart was 28 km [17 miles]. Whilst attacking the bombers I had flown in one direction only at a speed of approximately 360 km/h [225 mph]. It can be estimated that my speed was 340 km/h [210 mph] throughout the engagement. It takes 4 min 56 sec to travel 28 kilometres at that speed, so it can be concluded that the encounter took place over four to five minutes. I was airborne for 30 minutes in total.

'When analysing the results of the combat, there were several reasons for my success. My own training since May of the previous year, when I was posted to the fighter command, had been very thorough. The most important part was being sent to Käkisalmi gunnery camp, where I increased my hitting accuracy against aerial targets from eight per cent to 89 per cent, which was a record achievement with 300 rounds.

'I had been assigned aircraft FR-97 at Käkisalmi, and had subsequently flown it during the mobilisation and for more than a month of combat missions, so I was quite familiar with it by the time I engaged the seven Soviet bombers.

'Mechanic Ojala and both deputy mechanics had been with me since the mobilisation. I had instructed them in how I wanted my fighter to be set up, which meant that I did not have to adjust armament and pressure systems, evenness of the ammunition belts, cockpit glazing, etc. once I was in the air. My mechanics were very capable and thorough men.

'The guns of FR-97 were harmonised according to my liking. The streams of bullets converged at 130 metres [140 yd]. The rounds were chosen so that both wing guns had standard ammunition, the port fuselage weapon having incendiaries and the starboard one tracers. This choice served the purpose at that time, but better results were later

Pilots of LLv 24 in front of FR-110 at Joutseno in January 1940. They are, from left to right, Sgt Martti Alho, 2Lt Tapani Harmaja, 1Lts Jussi Räty and Veikko Karu, Maj Gustaf Magnusson and MSgt Sakari Ikonen. Visible behind them are WO Viktor Pyötsiä, 2Lt Iikka Törrönen, 1Lt Per Sovelius (obscured) and a war correspondent (J Sarvanto)

achieved by using incendiary or armour-piercing bullets in the faster-firing wing guns.

'The DB-3 bombers that I destroyed were probably not fitted with rubber self-sealing fuel tanks, which would explain their vulnerability. Also, the rear gunners did not have any armour protection. All DB and SB bombers that I later shot down appeared to be much harder to destroy.

'Local air surveillance and communications worked without any malfunctions, and without their service I probably could not have found my victims.

'Of the six bombers that I shot down, only a captain, who broke his leg, and a senior lieutenant survived. Both were interrogated at Kouvola air surveillance area centre. The captain said that his formation had been the same one that 1st Lt Sovelius had attacked in the morning, downing a bomber. Sovelius also later destroyed the DB-3 that escaped me, the aircraft crashing near Suursaari.

'Twenty-three bullet holes were counted in my aeroplane, including some caused by exploding ammunition. Most of the holes were in the wings, but my propeller had been hit in two of its three blades. Holes were also found in the engine, the underside of the fuselage and the radio cover behind the canopy. The engine had protected the instrument panel and cockpit from being hit.'

1Lt Sarvanto's exploits during this mission quickly became international news, for he had become the first 'ace in a mission' of World War 2.

Pilots of 4/LLv 24 crowd around the cockpit of a D.XXI at Joutseno in January 1940 for the benefit of a visiting war photographer. In the cockpit is 1Lt Per Sovelius, sat on the canopy is 2Lt Olli Mustonen and standing is 2Lt Iikka Törrönen. Typically for the Winter War, these three pilots flew more than 100 missions each (*J Sarvanto*)

From 7 January the weather turned very cold, with the temperature below -40°C almost daily. Both sides did very little flying for ten days as a result.

Although 17 January was also a very cold day, ten D.XXIs of LLv 24 scrambled, and at 1355 hrs they caught 25 SB bombers of 54th SBAP returning in three formations via the Karelian Isthmus. In just 25 minutes nine bombers were brought down and several more were damaged. Forty-eight hours later LLv 24 added two new aces to its ranks when both 1Lt Urho Nieminen and SSgt Kelpo Virta downed an SB bomber each over the Karelian Isthmus, taking their respective tallies to five.

Following these successes the air space over southeastern Finland became almost free of bombers. This was not the case further north, however, for on 20 January Detachment Luukkanen of LLv 24 engaged SB bombers of 21st DBAP north of Lake Ladoga both as they arrived and departed. D.XXI pilots succeeded in destroying five of them, with two being claimed by WO Viktor Pyötsiä and one by SSgt Pentti Tilli, both men thus becoming aces. Minutes later two I-16s appeared on the scene to chase the Finnish Fokkers away from the surviving SBs, and Tilli, in FR-107, was shot down and killed.

Later that same day 1Lt Tatu Huhanantti took off from Tampere in a D.XXI that had been under repair at the State Aircraft Factory. En route to his frontline base he met three SB bombers of 35th SBAP and quickly

shot down two of them before their escort of five I-153 'Chaikas' could intercede. The wrecks were easily found as the aeroplanes came down right alongside a railway line some 60 km (37 miles) north of Helsinki.

Upon landing FR-117 at Joroinen on 8 April 1940, MSgt Lauri Rautakorpi of 1/LLv 24 slid into a camouflaged barn. 'White 8' was normally assigned to Winter War ace 2Lt Olli Puhakka, who was on loan from LLv 26. Puhakka went on to score 46 victories and be awarded the Mannerheim Cross on 21 December 1944 (*J Dahl*)

FIGHTER COMBAT BAN

Although only two D.XXIs had been lost in combat since the Winter War commenced, and only one of these had been downed by Soviet fighters, there had been a number of close calls. Fearful of further losses, and fully aware that there were no attrition replacements available, LeR 2 CO Lt Col Richard Lorentz banned his pilots from searching out and engaging enemy fighters in aerial combat, insisting that only the bombers were to be attacked. As previously mentioned, the D.XXI was no match for the much more manoeuvrable I-153s and I-16s, which also enjoyed huge numerical superiority.

On 29 January Red Army artillery batteries accurately shelled Finnish positions on the Karelian Isthmus with the aid of spotters in a pair of venerable Polikarpov R-5 fire-control biplanes. Whilst still under fire, the Karelian Army commander contacted his counterpart in LeR 2 and requested that one of his fighters be scrambled so as to put a stop to this. 1Lt Jorma Karhunen of LLv 24 later described how this was done;

'At 1455 hrs I was ordered to take off with three other Fokkers and head for Summa, where we were to drive off or destroy two artillery fire-control R-5 aeroplanes. Five minutes later the Fokker *swarm* sped across the ice and took off. My wingman was WO Yrjö Turkka, while 2Lt Olli Mustonen led the other pair, with Sgt Tauno Kaarma as his wingman.

'As we headed for the Karelian Isthmus I worked out how best to engage the enemy spotting aircraft. They would flee the scene as soon as they heard word that Finnish fighters were approaching. Once we had gone they would pop up again. I decided to fool the Soviet fighter spotters.

'We flew along the west coast of Viipurinlahti just below the cloud base at 2000 metres [6,500 ft]. We continued south until we reached Koivisto, where we turned towards Summa. At this point I led the *swarm* into the clouds. As we approached Summa I headed out of the overcast in FR-80 so as to make sure that our "patients" were still there. There they were, circling and sending instructions to the artillery. They were still some

Cpl Onni Paronen was loaned by LLv 26 to LLv 24 during the Winter War, and he is seen here posing in front of FR-90 (which belonged to the 2nd Flight) in December 1939. In addition to his two Winter War victories, Paronen eventually gained another 8.5 kills flying Fiat G.50s and Bf 109Gs (*Finnish Aviation Museum*)

2Lt Iikka Törrönen of 4/LLv 24 rests between missions during the Winter War. His assigned aircraft was FR-104, and he claimed two shared aircraft destroyed with it. By the time he was shot down and killed on 2 May 1943, Törrönen's tally had reached 11 victories (*J Sarvanto*)

way away, so I quickly snuck back into the clouds. Three minutes seemed a long time, but I controlled myself. Then we bounced them out of the clouds.

'One R-5 was conveniently below us, and "Daddy" Turkka and I attacked together, firing simultaneously from above and behind. Moments later the wings collapsed after the fuselage had burst into flames. The flaming ball of fire came down between the lines. We then all fired at the other R-5 and it crashed beyond the frontlines. The job was done.

'We also managed to escape unscathed from the fierce anti-aircraft fire and return to our own side, which was a miracle.'

The State Aircraft Factory at Tampere was a frequent target for Soviet bombers, and local fighter defence was organised by test pilots, who were occasionally assisted by frontline pilots in the process of collecting repaired aircraft. Such was the case during the afternoon of 29 January, as reported by 2Lt Olli Puhakka;

'I had been on an interception with 1Lt Visapää, and we were about to land at Tampere airfield. He was 200 metres [220 yd] ahead of me, and almost above the runway, when we observed a large twin-engined aircraft flying a

31

course transverse to ours. 1Lt Visapää opened fire as the aircraft passed in front of him, but he was left behind when I commenced a climbing turn after the bomber. I was now 500-700 metres [550-760 yd] behind the aircraft, which was pulling away from me.

'My fighter was equipped with 20 mm cannon, and I started to fire short bursts at the enemy aeroplane in an attempt to slow it down. Although I initially shot below my target, my second burst hit the port engine and the third hit the starboard engine. Either one must have been damaged because I instantly caught up with the aeroplane, but now my guns refused to work. After making a few diving passes at the aeroplane I left it between Lempäälä and Viiala, assuming that 1Lt Visapää, who was flying off my starboard side, would finish it off. He, however, had lost it in a cloud shortly after my last pass.

'Fortunately, the bomber had been damaged enough that the crew force-landed it at Urjala and were captured. We awaited word from our troops as to whether my cannon shells or 1Lt Visapää's machine gun rounds had brought the aircraft down.

'I was flying FR-76 on this occasion, which was equipped with a 20 mm cannon in each wing, although only one weapon was working. I used all 18 rounds in the drum. I had also fired 60-70 rounds from my two fuselage machine guns before their synchronising gear failed.

The downed DB-3M was from 53rd DBAP, and it had clearly been struck by several cannon shells. The victory was 2Lt Olli Puhakka's.

The following day LLv 24 lost another D.XXI when 2nd Flight leader 1Lt Jaakko Vuorela, flying FR-78, crashed to his death in poor weather at Ruokolahti. The flight was taken over by 1Lt Leo Ahola, the formation duly being called Detachment Ahola, while 1Lt Jorma Karhunen led the 2nd Flight.

By the end of January there were 28 serviceable D.XXIs in LLv 24, and at this point in the conflict ten of the squadron's 'hired' pilots returned to their original unit, LLv 26, which had just begun to receive ex-Royal Air Force Gloster Gladiator IIs. The January score for the Fokker fighters was 34 enemy aircraft shot down.

ESCORTS

By early February the Soviet Union had concentrated two armies along the edges of the Karelian Isthmus. On the Northwestern Front, 7th Army held the western side, while 13th Army was dug in to the east. Combined, these armies had 23 divisions of infantry, six armoured brigades and two detached armoured battalions at their disposal. Their task was to break through the Finnish defences and advance to Helsinki. Thirty aviation regiments and the Baltic Fleet Air Forces – just over 2000 aircraft – protected the armies from above.

After a lull in the action on the frontline, on 1 February the Soviet Union launched the second phase of its offensive on the Karelian Isthmus. Other fronts were left as they were, all available manpower being concentrated here as the Red Army searched for a breakthrough in the Finnish line. The homeland bomber offensive was switched to immediate support of the attack, and large fighter formations started patrolling over the frontline and just beyond it. (text continues on page 47)

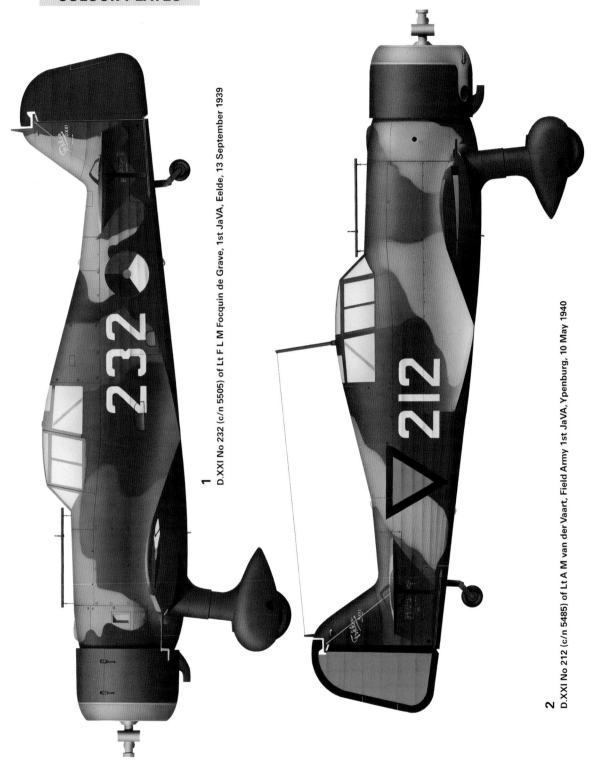

1
D.XXI No 232 (c/n 5505) of Lt F L M Focquin de Grave, 1st JaVA, Eelde, 13 September 1939

2
D.XXI No 212 (c/n 5485) of Lt A M van der Vaart, Field Army 1st JaVA, Ypenburg, 10 May 1940

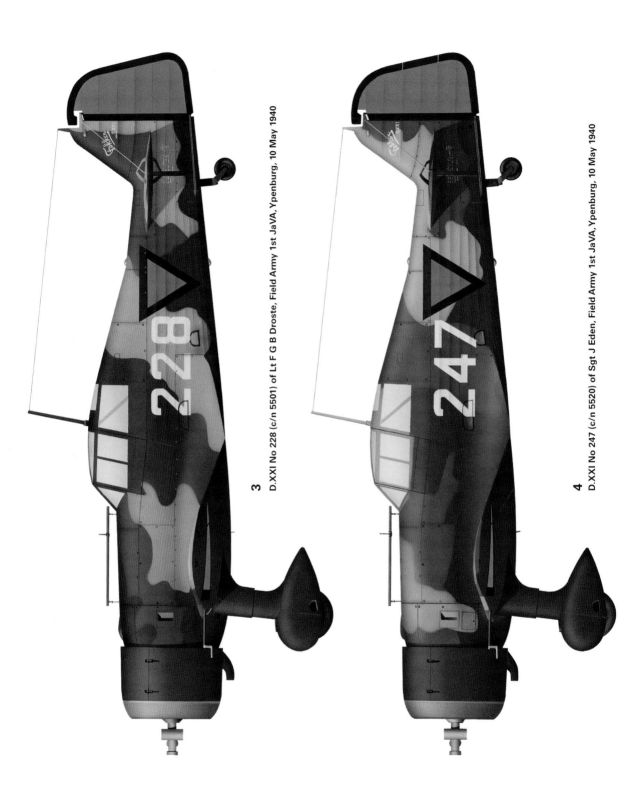

3
D.XXI No 228 (c/n 5501) of Lt F G B Droste, Field Army 1st JaVA, Ypenburg, 10 May 1940

4
D.XXI No 247 (c/n 5520) of Sgt J Eden, Field Army 1st JaVA, Ypenburg, 10 May 1940

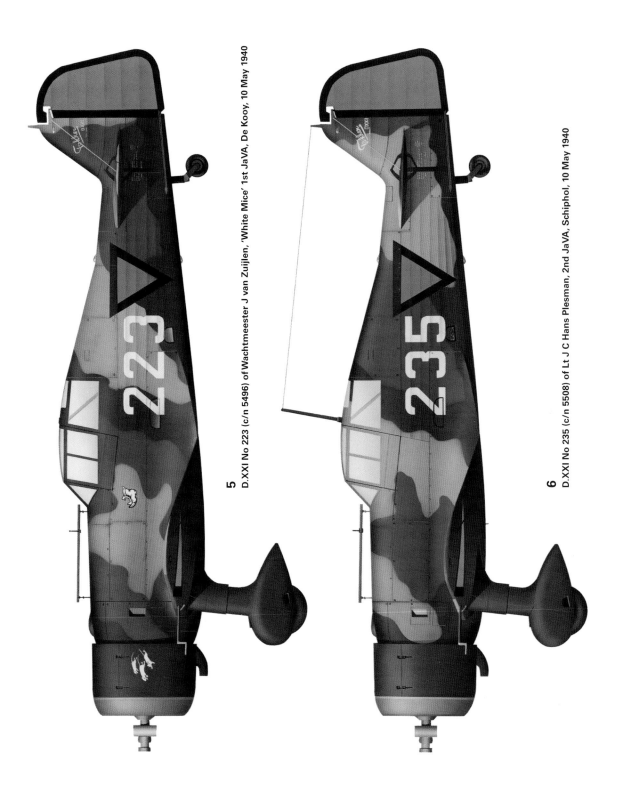

5

D.XXI No 223 (c/n 5496) of Wachtmeester J van Zuijlen, 'White Mice' 1st JaVA, De Kooy, 10 May 1940

6

D.XXI No 235 (c/n 5508) of Lt J C Hans Plesman, 2nd JaVA, Schiphol, 10 May 1940

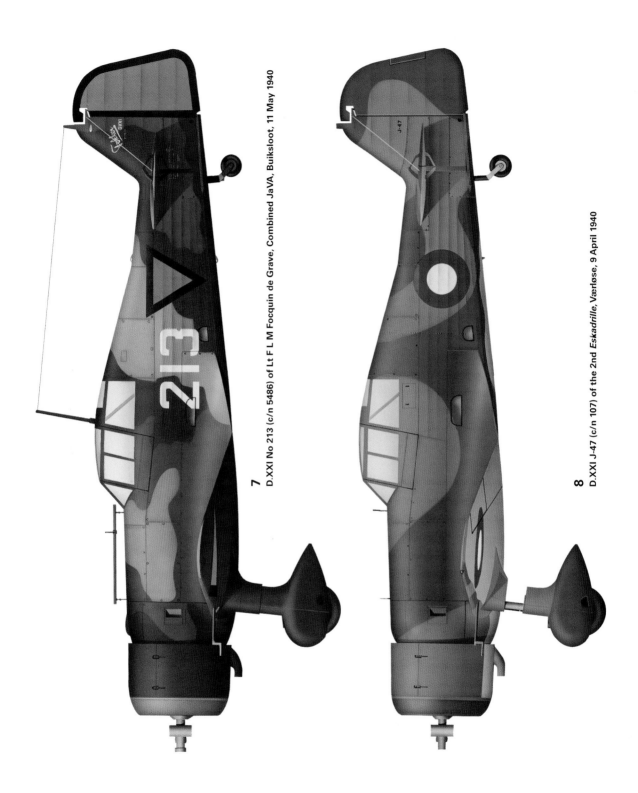

7

D.XXI No 213 (c/n 5486) of Lt F L M Focquin de Grave, Combined JaVA, Buiksloot, 11 May 1940

8

D.XXI J-47 (c/n 107) of the 2nd *Eskadrille*, Værløse, 9 April 1940

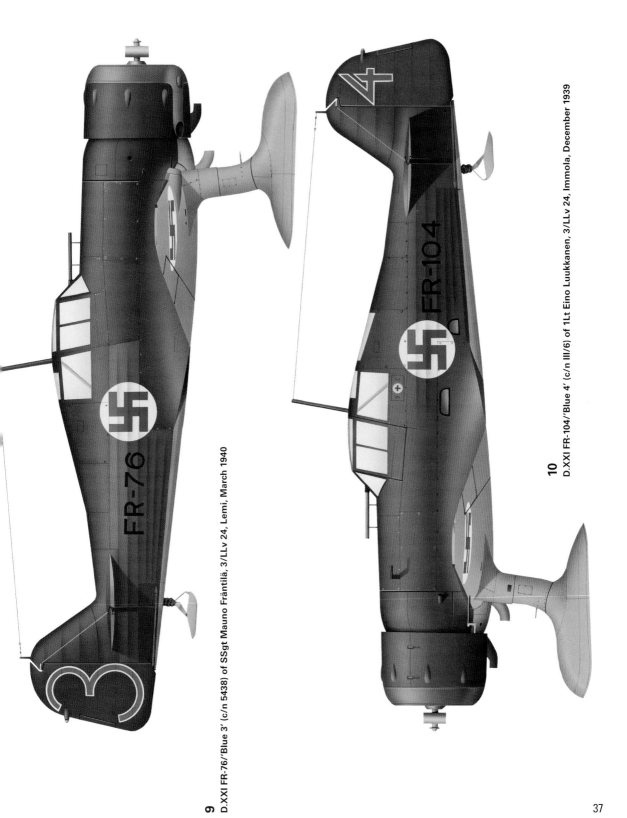

9

D.XXI FR-76/'Blue 3' (c/n 5438) of SSgt Mauno Fräntilä, 3/LLv 24, Lemi, March 1940

10

D.XXI FR-104/'Blue 4' (c/n III/6) of 1Lt Eino Luukkanen, 3/LLv 24, Immola, December 1939

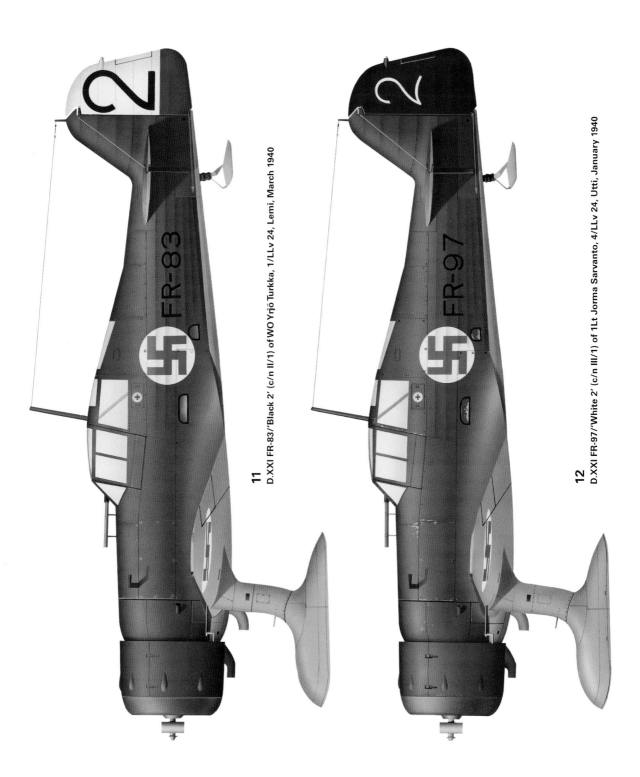

11
D.XXI FR-83/'Black 2' (c/n II/1) of WO Yrjö Turkka, 1/LLv 24, Lemi, March 1940

12
D.XXI FR-97/'White 2' (c/n III/1) of 1Lt Jorma Sarvanto, 4/LLv 24, Utti, January 1940

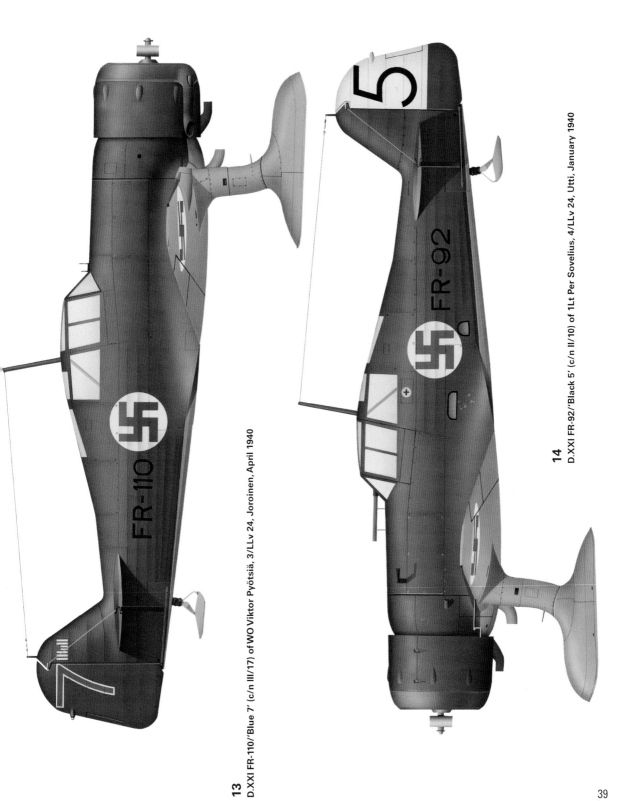

13

D.XXI FR-110/'Blue 7' (c/n III/17) of WO Viktor Pyötsiä, 3/LLv 24, Joroinen, April 1940

14

D.XXI FR-92/'Black 5' (c/n II/10) of 1Lt Per Sovelius, 4/LLv 24, Utti, January 1940

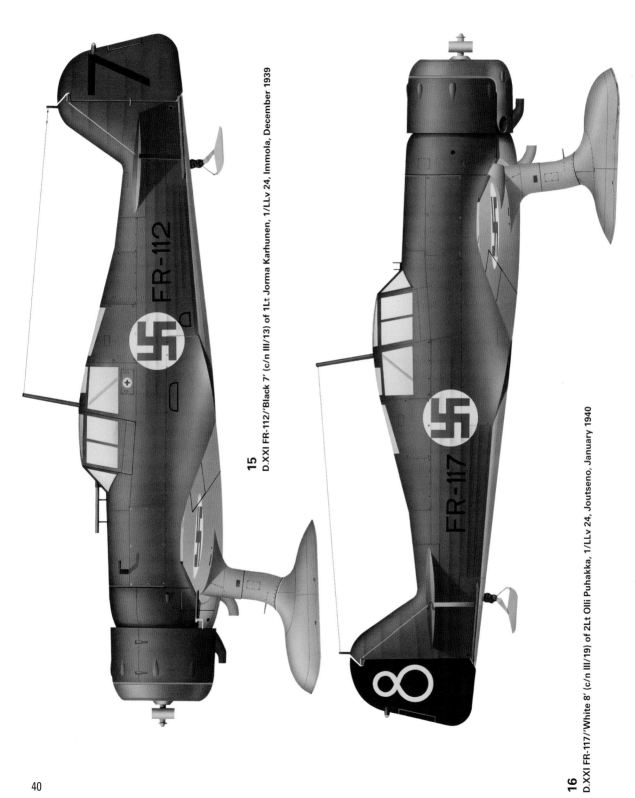

15
D.XXI FR-112/'Black 7' (c/n III/13) of 1Lt Jorma Karhunen, 1/LLv 24, Immola, December 1939

16
D.XXI FR-117/'White 8' (c/n III/19) of 2Lt Olli Puhakka, 1/LLv 24, Joutseno, January 1940

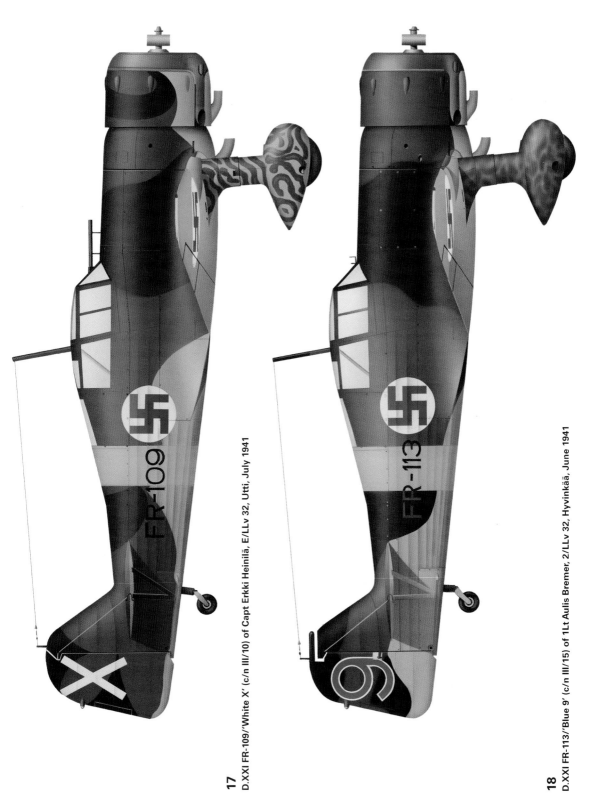

17
D.XXI FR-109/'White X' (c/n III/10) of Capt Erkki Heinilä, E/LLv 32, Utti, July 1941

18
D.XXI FR-113/'Blue 9' (c/n III/15) of 1Lt Aulis Bremer, 2/LLv 32, Hyvinkää, June 1941

19

D.XXI FR-95/'White 5' (c/n II/13) of SSgt Paul Salminen, 1/LLv 32, Utti, July 1941

20

D.XXI FR-114/'White 2' (c/n III/21) of 1Lt Veikko Evinen, 1/LLv 32, Utti, June 1941

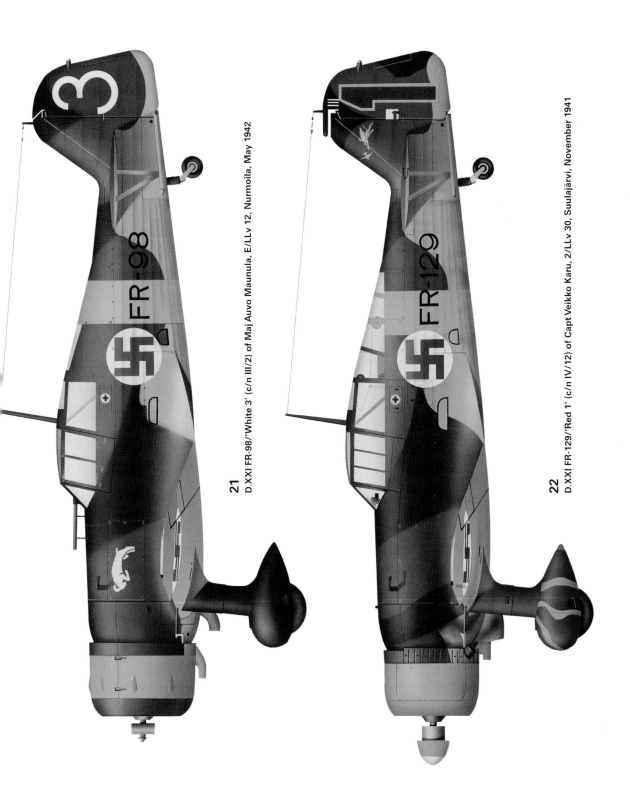

21
D.XXI FR-98/'White 3' (c/n III/2) of Maj Auvo Maunula, E/LLv 12, Nurmoila, May 1942

22
D.XXI FR-129/'Red 1' (c/n IV/12) of Capt Veikko Karu, 2/LLv 30, Suulajärvi, November 1941

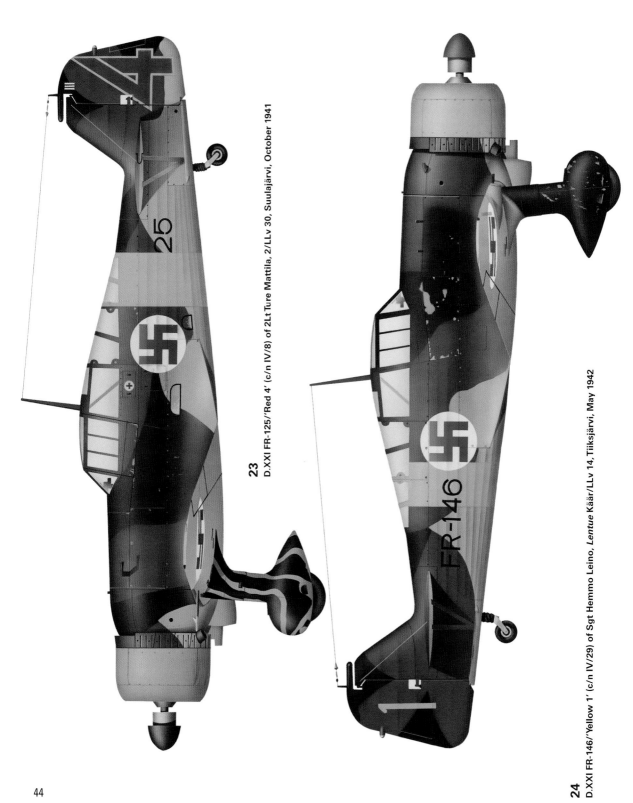

23
D.XXI FR-125/'Red 4' (c/n IV/8) of 2Lt Ture Mattila, 2/LLv 30, Suulajärvi, October 1941

24
D.XXI FR-146/'Yellow 1' (c/n IV/29) of Sgt Hemmo Leino, *Lentue Käär*/LLv 14, Tiiksjärvi, May 1942

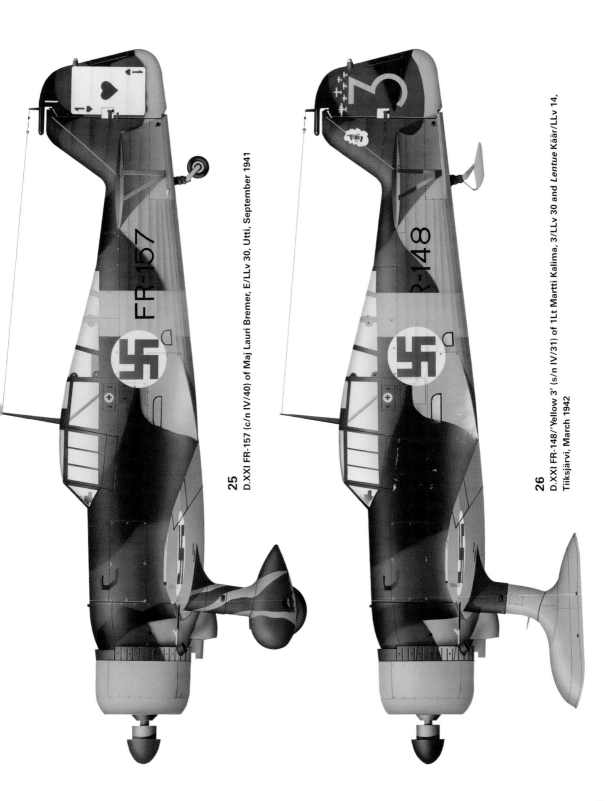

25
D.XXI FR-157 (c/n IV/40) of Maj Lauri Bremer, E/LLv 30, Utti, September 1941

26
D.XXI FR-148/'Yellow 3' (s/n IV/31) of 1Lt Martti Kalima, 3/LLv 30 and *Lentue* Käär/LLv 14, Tiiksjärvi, March 1942

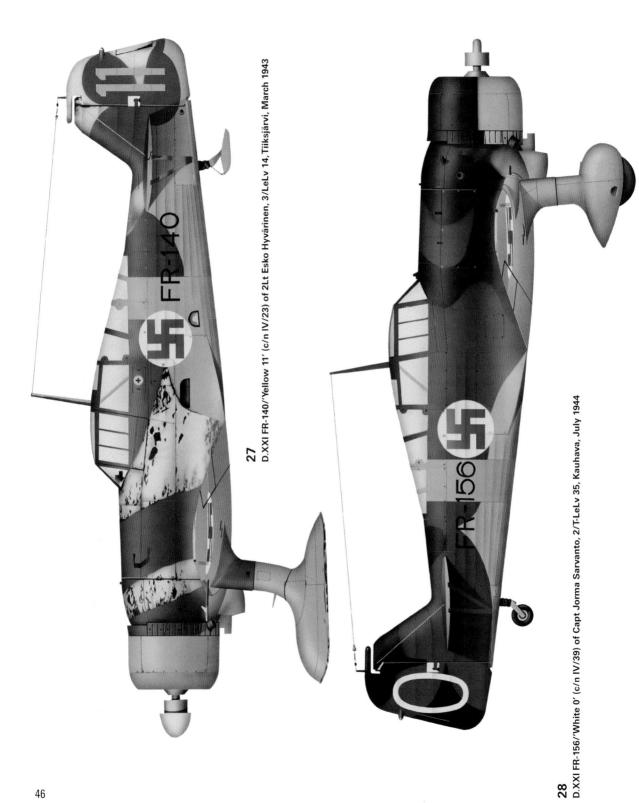

27
D.XXI FR-140/'Yellow 11' (c/n IV/23) of 2Lt Esko Hyvärinen, 3/LeLv 14, Tiiksjärvi, March 1943

28
D.XXI FR-156/'White 0' (c/n IV/39) of Capt Jorma Sarvanto, 2/T-LeLv 35, Kauhava, July 1944

Pilots of LLv 24 in front of FR-95 in February 1940. They are, from left to right, 2Lts Olli Mustonen and Iikka Törrönen, WO Yrjö Turkka, 1Lt Per Sovelius (seated), Sgt Eero Kinnunen, MSgt Sakari Ikonen, 2Lt Toivo Vuorimaa and Sgts Martt Alho and Lasse Heikinaro (sat on the wing at right) (*J Sarvanto*)

On 2 February LLv 24 lost a D.XXI and its pilot, Danish volunteer 1Lt Frits Rasmussen, to 25th IAP fighters. That same day Detachment Ahola flew to Turku, on the southwest coast, to protect the main Finnish port and prevent Soviet bombers flying northbound along the west coast.

On the 3rd 1Lt Jorma Sarvanto of LLv 24 claimed his tenth kill, shooting down a DB-3M bomber of 51st DBAP at Nuijamaa, in southeastern Finland. In the west four Fokkers bounced three DB-3s of 10th AB (*Aviatsionnaya Diviziya* – Aviation Brigade) and sent them down into the Turku archipelago, 2Lt Pekka Kokko claiming two of the bombers.

Thereafter, LLv 24 flew myriad escort missions daily, protecting troops and motorised transports from Soviet bomber attacks. Opportunities for claims became fewer, but some combats still occurred. On 9 February, for example, the D.XXI pilots flew 31 interception sorties over the Karelian Isthmus and claimed two R-5s shot down. The following day the 4th Flight of LLv 24 attacked a large bomber formation over Lappeenranta, but the equally numerous fighter escort handled the situation well and shot down the D.XXI of MSgt Sakri Ikonen, who was wounded in the process. Big claims were now history for the Fokker pilots, with daily scores rarely exceeding three bombers at the most. Losses also started to accumulate.

On 11 February the Red Army launched a new attack on the Karelian Isthmus in the Summa sector, which three days later would lead to a breakthrough in the main defensive line. Seventy-one sorties were flown by LLv 24 on 13 February in an attempt to protect Finnish Army troops struggling to hold the line, but the unit failed to gain any results in combat. The following day the Soviet 7th Army forced the Finnish infantry to withdraw four kilometres from their main defensive line. LLv 24 flew 69 sorties protecting troops that had been urgently transferred to the Karelian Isthmus to repel 7th Army. Two bombers from a 19-aircraft strong 48th SBAP formation were shot down near Lappeenranta as they attempted to attack the reinforcements.

On several occasions on 17 February Kouvola, an important railway and road junction, was the main target for Soviet bombers. During the course of the day LLv 24 managed to scatter two 30-aircraft-strong bomber formations over the immediate rear of the Karelian Isthmus front. In 26 combats three bombers were shot down.

When more than 300 aircraft targeted Vyborg on 18 February, LLv 24 flew 65 interception sorties and claimed three bombers shot down. The next day large formations of bombers escorted by numerous fighters flew over the Karelian Isthmus, and LLv 24 flew 60 interception missions, claiming two bombers destroyed. Near Käkisalmi 25th IAP fighters shot down and killed Danish volunteer 1Lt Erhard Frijs, who was flying FR-80.

7th Army broke through the intermediary line on the Karelian Isthmus on 20 February 1940, although its advance was temporarily stopped the next day. All but overwhelmed by reports of 480 sightings of Soviet bombers, pilots from LLv 24 flew 59 intercept sorties. They failed to prevent the bombardment of Elisenvaara railway junction, which delayed the transfer of a Finnish Army division to the Karelian Isthmus.

Many fighter bases and forward landing grounds came under almost continuous attack by patrolling Soviet fighters on 21 February. In return, LLv 24 claimed two bombers and two fighters shot down.

Five days later large formations of Soviet bombers attacked Immola, LLv 24's main base. The D.XXI pilots flew 47 interception missions in response, trying to engage formations as large as 60 aircraft, but the Soviet escort fighters made it impossible for them to attack the bombers. Sgt Tauno Kaarma, flying D.XXI FR-85, was wounded when 68th IAP fighters shot his aircraft down in flames near Immola.

The last day of February proved to be the worst for the Finnish fighter arm, with Soviet fighters carrying out a series of air raids on the bases of LLvs 24 and 26. Three weeks earlier Detachment Luukkanen of LLv 24 had moved to Ruokolahti, and two Gladiator flights of LLv 26 were put under its command there. On the morning of the 29th 68th IAP fighters shot down a Gladiator. At noon it was announced that a bomber formation was approaching Ruokolahti, but it turned out to be six 'Chaikas' and 18 'Ratas', again from 68th IAP, which took the Gladiators completely by surprise as they were taking off. Three were immediately destroyed, and in the low-level combat that ensued two more Gladiators and D.XXI

The leader of 3/LLv 24, 1Lt Eino Luukkanen, poses in the cockpit of his D.XXI during the Winter War. He scored 2.5 aerial victories during the conflict, then went on to increase his tally to 54 flying Brewsters and Bf 109Gs. These victories ultimately earned Luukkanen the Mannerheim Cross on 18 June 1944 (*E Luukkanen*)

FR-94, piloted by 6.5-victory ace 1Lt Tatu Huhanantti, were brought down and their pilots killed. Only one I-16 was claimed in return, and another hit trees while manoeuvring at low altitude.

During February LLv 24 had claimed 27 aircraft destroyed, but at the end of the month it had only 22 serviceable Fokkers on strength.

GROUND ATTACK

Having halted their advance at the rearmost Finnish defence line on the Karelian Isthmus, southeast of Vyborg, the Soviet armies then decided to attack the seemingly vulnerable rear areas of the defensive positions by crossing the frozen Viipurinlahti (Gulf of Vyborg). In other sectors of the frontline the communist advance had come to an end too, and north of Lake Ladoga besieged elements of the Red Army, cut off and facing a slow starvation, fiercely held onto their encircled enclaves. The Soviets tried to advance to the rear of the Finnish defensive line in this sector and help break the encirclements, but these efforts proved fruitless.

In the rear of the Karelian Isthmus Front, LeR 2's bases came under continuous air attack from both fighters and bombers. In an effort to remain operational the flights of LLv 24 continued to use several forward landing grounds and frozen lakes.

On 3 March the Red Army started to advance across the frozen Gulf of Vyborg. At 1400 hrs Gladiator reconnaissance pilots of LLv 12 sent alarming reports that the first units were near the coast at Vilajoki, in the rear of the main defence line. By the afternoon of 4 March Soviet troops had managed to cross the gulf and form a bridgehead at Vilaniemi and Häränpääniemi. Troops and armoured columns flowed across the ice from Pulliniemi and Tuppura. All *Ilmavoimat* units were ordered to repel this invasion at the rear. For LLv 24 and other fighter units it meant continuous strafing missions against enemy troops, supply columns and vehicles as they crossed the ice towards the bridgeheads.

The Gulf of Vyborg also drew the attention of Soviet fighters, which attempted to protect the troops exposed on the ice. Capt Eino Luukkanen of LLv 24 led several strafing missions on 5 March, and here he describes one such sortie conducted in the early evening:

'I broke radio silence and ordered the formation [of 15 D.XXIs] out of the clouds. Now we were playing with the enemy by approaching them from their direction. I banked to the left and led the formation into a dive. There seemed to be no lack of targets because the four-kilometre distance between Tuppura and Vilaniemi was full of troop columns, cars, trucks and tanks.

'An I-16 squadron circled above Uuras, and another fighter unit was on the other side of the gulf over Ristiniemi. I continued my shallow dive, as the sooner we strafed the better for us. We were only a kilometre away from the nearest targets when the air around us filled with flak and tracer rounds. White and black clouds of smoke from exploding shells dotted the sky, and these in turn attracted the attention of enemy fighters.

'My first burst hit an infantry column, my second a line of trucks and, finally, my third two tanks. The bullets of our rifle-calibre machine guns did not seem to have any effect on the tanks, as I saw the tracers bounce

Four pilots of LLv 24's 3rd Flight amuse themselves at Ruokolahti in late February 1940. Seated is the flight leader, Capt Eino Luukkanen, standing is MSgt Ilmari Juutilainen and Sgts Jalo Dahl and Martti Alho are on the wing (*J Dahl*)

off their armour plating. After my strafing run I looked back to make sure that the rest of the formation had followed my example.

'I quickly led my pilots away to the west, initially at low level, before banking north towards our airfield. By following this course it was hoped that the enemy would not discover our location should a Soviet aircraft have tried to tail us.'

On 6 March LLv 24 flew 18 strafing sorties against men and materiel of the Red Army out on the ice of the Gulf of Vyborg. The next day LLv 24 completed no fewer than 43 strafing sorties in the same area. By now this mission had become much deadlier, however, as the Soviets had placed anti-aircraft artillery units on both sides of the ice roads, in addition to mounting continuous air patrols by large fighter formations – often whole regiments, numbering 50 aircraft.

Peace negotiations began in Moscow on 8 March. By then Soviet forces had advanced to the Vyborg-Helsinki main road. During the previous week the ice over the Gulf of Vyborg had been swept clean of the Red Army thanks to determined attacks by the *Ilmavoimat*, inflicting heavy casualties on the invaders. The advance on Finland had also been stopped and Vyborg remained untaken. The D.XXI pilots of LLv 24 had flown 154 strafing sorties, claimed one I-16 shot down and lost FR-76, piloted by future ace SSgt 'Manu' Fräntilä, who was injured when he crash-landed in no-man's land.

On 13 March the Winter War ended at 1100 hrs with the enforcement of the peace agreement negotiated in Moscow. Finland had to give up vast areas of its land to the Soviet Union – most of the Karelian territory and smaller areas further north. This was hard on the Finns, as Soviet troops had not even come close to occupying these areas. However, Finnish independence was preserved, albeit at a very high cost.

From a Soviet perspective, Stalin was willing to agree to the peace treaty, rather than continuing to wage war, for two main reasons.

Above left
Photographed at Siikakangas with its engine running in late May 1940, FR-108 of LLv 32 still wears the markings used by Capt Eino Luukkanen when he was leading 3/LLv 24 during the Winter War. Flying 'Blue 6', he scored 1.5 of the 2.5 victories he claimed in that conflict (*Finnish Air Force Museum*)

Above right
FR-83 of LLv 32 was also photographed at Siikakangas in late May 1940. WO Yrjö Turkka had been flying this machine (in these markings) with 1/LLv 24 a few months earlier when he scored 4.5 aerial victories during the Winter War. He went on to enjoy success both with the Brewster and Bf 109G, and his final score reached 17.5 kills (*Finnish Air Force Museum*)

D.XXI FR-76 of 3/LLv 24 was so badly damaged in combat on 5 March 1940 that Sgt Mauno Fräntilä was forced to crash-land between the lines at Virolahti, on the north shore of the Gulf of Viipuri. Although the aeroplane then became a target for Finnish mortar fire, the Soviets managed to salvage FR-76 and put it on display in the Spartak movie theatre in Leningrad shortly after the Winter War had ended (*via C-F Geust*)

The second-highest-scoring aeroplane in the Winter War was FR-110, and it was used by the conflict's third-ranking ace, WO Viktor Pyötsiä of 3/LLv 24, to claim all of his 7.5 victories. Marked throughout this period as 'Blue 7', it is the only D.XXI known to have carried victory bars from the 1939-40 conflict. On 8 April 1940 the fighter's port ski came loose in the air, but 2Lt Olli Mustonen successfully landed FR-110 at Joroinen (*J Dahl*)

Firstly, the level of resistance by Finnish armed forces was far beyond the prewar estimates calculated by the Red Army, which faced further embarrassing losses on the battlefield should the war have been allowed to continue. Secondly, the Soviet Union did not want Britain or France joining the fight on the Finnish side. Both of these nations had promised to send huge numbers of troops to Finland had peace negotiations been unsuccessful. Of course this was very much a hollow threat, as moving half a million men was unrealistic, but the flow of aircraft to the *Ilmavoimat* from both countries had been continuing for several weeks, and more kept coming.

From a Finnish standpoint, the government understood that the resistance to the Soviet invasion could not be maintained for much longer – a fact that had obviously escaped the USSR. It was also realised that foreign help would consist of little more than obsolescent aircraft and other supplies that could be flown in, although some in Helsinki naively believed that international troops would arrive. Accepting the severe terms of peace would save most of the country.

There is also some evidence that Germany, which was officially neutral throughout this period, had secretly recommended to the Finnish

FR-116 of 5/LLv 24, parked at Joroinen in early April 1940, displays a 'Blue 4' on its rudder. The fighter was regularly flown by 2Lt Kauko Linnamaa, who had been loaned to the unit by LLv 26. Flying this machine, he shared in the destruction of a DB-3M bomber on 21 December 1939 (*J Dahl*)

FR-105/'White 5' of 5/LLv 24 at Joroinen in April 1940. This aircraft was assigned to Sgt Eero Kinnunen, although he claimed all of his 3.5 Winter War kills in FR-109. On 19 April 1940 LLv 24 exchanged its D.XXIs for Brewsters, the latter fighters being transferred to the unit from LLv 32 (*Finnish Air Force Museum*)

FR-95 of LLv 32 at Siikakangas in June 1940. After suffering damage during a landing accident, this machine was delivered to 4/LLv 24 on 3 February 1940 and assigned to MSgt Lasse Heikinaro, who claimed three victories with it. This aircraft became 'Black 6' with LLv 24, the unit having introduced its own tactical numbers by September 1940

government that it accept the harsh peace terms. All lost territory would soon be taken back, and much more – the German invasion of Denmark and Norway was only four weeks away. Certainly, plans for the invasion of the Soviet Union already existed in the minds of Germany's military leaders.

SUMMARY

LLv 24 had gone into the Winter War with 35 serviceable D.XXIs and ended it with 22. The unit had flown 2388 sorties and claimed 120 aircraft shot down, of which 100 were bombers. It lost 11 aircraft to all causes – nine in combat, one to Finnish anti-aircraft fire and one in a flying accident. Seven pilots had been killed. All these figures include the claims and losses of Fokker pilots 'on loan' from LLv 26.

The D.XXI had proven itself to be a very reliable interceptor, and its simple construction enabled the aircraft to be kept operational even in the most severe winter conditions – daily temperatures throughout the conflict were usually -30ºC, and on several days down to -40ºC. The D.XXI bore the brunt of fighter operations for the *Ilmavoimat*, as the Gladiator IIs became operational on 2 February and claimed 37 aerial victories, the MS.406s drew first blood on 17 February and were credited with 14 kills and Fiat G.50 pilots claimed their first successes on 26 February 1940, finally achieving 11 victories.

The *Ilmavoimat* was credited with 207 aircraft shot down and Finnish flak batteries claimed a further 314, making a total of 521 aircraft destroyed. Contemporary Soviet records released at the time showed a loss of just 261 combat aircraft. However, recent figures gleaned by historians trawling through the Russian archives actually show that Soviet units lost 579 aircraft during the Winter War – well in line with Finnish claims.

WAR IN THE WEST

British and French plans to send troops to support Finland, mentioned in the previous chapter, were not without an ulterior motive, as these troops would have had to travel through neutral Norway and Sweden, thus cutting off the supply of Swedish iron ore to Germany, which largely passed through Narvik. On 8 April 1940, with Finland no longer an excuse for the movement of troops through Scandinavia, the Royal Navy started minelaying in Norwegian waters, hoping for a German response that would allow them to occupy the Norwegian port. The Germans got there first, however, as an invasion fleet was already sailing for Norway.

As a stepping-stone in a logistically challenging operation, Denmark was included in the German plans. That country's weak defences were not mobilised and were unprepared, and its D.XXI squadron was no exception. Denmark's first Fokker fighter built by the Kløvermarken workshops had not been flown until August 1939. By April 1940 only the tenth, and final, aircraft was still unflown, although the Fokker-built pair were still awaiting conversion to operational standard. The other nine machines had been delivered to Army Aviation's 2nd *Eskadrille*, but both the unit and its aircraft were not fully operational. The Madsen cannon were still missing from the wings, so armament comprised only two machine guns, and radios had not been fitted. Worse still, not much flying had been done in the harsh winter, and even in the first week of April only six flying hours were logged by the D.XXIs, at least two aircraft being unserviceable.

When Operation *Weserübung* began on 9 April, Army Aviation was still concentrated at Værløse airfield, near Copenhagen, with its Fokker C.Vs and D.XXIs and Gloster Gauntlets. At the crack of dawn Messerschmitt Bf 110s of I./ZG I took off from Barth on Germany's Baltic coast. Led by *Gruppenkommandeur* Hauptmann Wolfgang Falck, who had become an ace during the first months of the war, two squadrons flew towards the coast of Zealand at low altitude, pulled up to locate Værløse and at 0520 hrs, with the rising sun on their backs, attacked the airfield, which had received word of German landings in the capital just ten minutes earlier.

Falck shot down a Fokker C.V (*not* a D.XXI) that was just taking off, killing its crew, while the other Bf 110s strafed the flightlines and taxiing aircraft. Although the anti-aircraft artillery opened up, Army Aviation's entire fleet of 25 operational aircraft was wiped out in one stroke, including three D.XXIs practically destroyed and three damaged. Just one month later ZG I was to encounter more serious opposition from the D.XXI over Holland.

Following Denmark's instant surrender, the country was initially

A Danish D.XXI in flight near its Værløse base, outside Copenhagen, in the early spring of 1940. The upper sections of the undercarriage leg fairings have been removed to prevent the accumulation of ice during a particularly harsh winter that kept the 2nd *Eskadrille* from working-up on its new equipment (*T Postma*)

put under a lenient occupation with self-rule, and while its aviation forces were grounded, the Kløvermarken workshops restarted work on the D.XXIs for future use. Just one of the heavily damaged aircraft was written off, with the remaining 11 airframes being rebuilt, repaired or completed and then stored, only to be confiscated by the Germans in 1943. The Luftwaffe appears to have used these aircraft as glider- or target-tugs for some time.

Danish pilots were to fly in the D.XXI no more, and the only Danes to score victories or, indeed, to see combat in the Dutch fighter were Erhard Frijs and Frits Rasmussen – the two volunteers who had been killed while fighting for Finland during the Winter War.

Denmark's D.XXI squadron was wiped out without a fight at Værløse by Wolfgang Falck's strafing Bf 110s. Although three D.XXIs were practically destroyed, all but one of them were rebuilt by the Danes, only to be confiscated by the Germans (*Royal Danish Air Force*)

WAR COMES TO HOLLAND

In Holland in early April 1940, while the 2nd JaVA was still at Eelde in the northeast of the country, fresh redeployments saw the D.XXIs of the Field Army 1st JaVA, now based at Eindhoven in the southeast, replace the 'White Mice' 1st JaVA, which had redeployed to Teuge, a minor airfield near Deventer in the central east.

News of the German invasions of Denmark and Norway shook the Dutch authorities, however, and the three D.XXI units received urgent orders to move to the defensible west of the country. Lorries were commandeered on the spot by the 'White Mice' 1st JaVA, which then headed for De Kooy naval airfield, where it had been based during the November alert. The 2nd JaVA went to Schiphol and the Field Army 1st JaVA to Ypenburg, the airport of The Hague.

The general alert was ended on 15 April, but the fighter units now stayed put at the western airfields. A final known peacetime encounter with the Luftwaffe took place on 4 May, when pilots Van Overvest and Bosch of the 'White Mice' 1st JaVA fired at a trespassing bomber that managed to escape. Another predicted invasion date, 8 May, passed uneventfully, but the next day the Dutch military attaché to Berlin, Maj Sas, received word from his German informants that Hitler had boarded his train to the Western Front. Operation *Fall Gelb* was about to begin.

D.XXIs of the Field Army 1st JaVA sit on the ramp in front of camouflaged buildings at Ypenburg, the airport of The Hague. Aircraft No 247 was Sgt Jaap Eden's mount. He damaged a Bf 110 with it, but subsequently landed amidst a ground battle that caused the destruction of his aircraft (*via F Gerdessen*)

Even though Holland was something of a sideshow in the German offensive, the Luftwaffe is believed to have employed some 400 fighters, 200 bombers and 100 reconnaissance aircraft against the Dutch on 10 May, as well as the bulk of the Junkers Ju 52/3m transport fleet. Germany's novel airborne troops were to capture key

bridges in the Rotterdam–Dordrecht area, allowing an armoured spearhead to enter the country's western heartland from the weakly defended south. An even quicker victory was hoped for, though, with a second airborne operation directly targeting the Dutch government in The Hague.

From around 0200 hrs local time on 10 May (0240 hrs GMT, 0340 hrs Berlin time – Holland had its own time, and daylight saving was not observed), Dutch airspace was violated by large formations of German aircraft. Both Army Aviation and the D.XXI were ill-equipped for night flying, however. The German machines continued westward, suggesting operations against England, but turned back over the North Sea and attacked at first light, destroying some Dutch aircraft on the ground – including G.I fighters of the 4th JaVA at Bergen. No D.XXIs were initially destroyed on the ground, and 28 scrambled from De Kooy, Schiphol and Ypenburg. The order of battle for the three D.XXI squadrons was as follows;

Field Army 1st JaVA – Ypenburg (The Hague)
1st flight – three D.XXIs (Lt Ruijs de Perez)
2nd flight – three D.XXIs (Lt Steen)
3rd flight – two D.XXIs (Lt Droste)

'White Mice' 1st JaVA – De Kooy (Den Helder)
1st flight ('Kleuter') – three D.XXIs (Lt Focquin de Grave)
2nd flight ('Mina') – three D.XXIs (Lt Van der Stok)
3rd flight ('Herman') – three D.XXIs (Lt Doppenberg)
4th flight ('Petrus') – two D.XXIs (Lt Huddleston Slater)

2nd JaVA – Schiphol (Amsterdam)
1st flight – three D.XXIs (Lt Plesman)
2nd flight – three D.XXIs (Lt Sitter)
3rd flight – three D.XXIs (Lt Bodaan)

FIELD ARMY 1st JaVA

Ypenburg was attacked by several formations of He 111 bombers from I./KG 4, accompanied by Bf 110s of II./ZG I. Then swarms of Ju 52/3ms appeared, dropping parachutists and landing airborne troops on Ypenburg and the other Hague airfields, Ockenburg and Valkenburg. The first wave of Heinkels missed their target, allowing the eight serviceable D.XXIs of the Field Army 1st JaVA to scramble, followed by the Douglas 8A attack aircraft of the Field Army 3rd JaVA which, flown as fighters, were shot out of the sky in a matter of minutes. The D.XXI unit was also virtually annihilated in chaotic air and ground combats, but not without destroying several German aircraft.

Upon takeoff, Lt Govert Steen's flight spotted a formation of He 111s that had just missed their airfield. Steen's machine guns would not cock, however, and he returned to Ypenburg, followed by his two wingmen, who did not have radios. Steen took Sgt Linzel's aircraft and took off again, with Lt Van der Vaart. A pneumatic valve switch fixed the cocking problem, and Jan Linzel took to the air in the leader's aircraft as bombs rained down on the airfield. After climbing to 10,000 ft Linzel got onto the tail of a Bf 110 and set one of its engines on fire. He then chased a formation of Heinkels and emptied his guns into one of the bombers, before being hit by fire from a second Bf 110, a 20 mm shell penetrating his thigh. Linzel was able to bail out of his D.XXI and pull his parachute ripcord before losing consciousness. He was eventually hospitalised.

Govert Steen clashed with several German aircraft and, unable to reach a safe airfield, landed on the Hague beach of Kijkduin, where he took an early city tram. He failed to convince his fellow passengers that their country was now at war! The D.XXI was destroyed later in the day, apparently by Dutch naval gunfire, as Ju 52/3ms had also landed on the beach.

Van der Vaart, who had lost sight of his leader, pursued and shot down a Do 17Z reconnaissance aircraft of Aufkl.St. 7 Fl.Div, which crashed near Wilnis after the crew bailed out. Having run out of fuel, Van der Vaart managed to glide into Schiphol.

The Field Army 1st JaVA's commander, Lt Boy Ruijs de Perez, found that his guns, too, did not work, but he chose to stay with his wingmen, Sgts Kiel and Eden, until he was wounded in the arm and made a crash landing. Guus Kiel recalled;

'We started chasing and attacking the approaching aircraft, Junkers and Heinkels and the whole caboodle. And the blokes in the Junkers fired from all the windows. They fired tracers, too, which flashed through the sky. Yet I wasn't scared. I felt safe behind my engine. I kept firing and firing. I shot an engine of a Ju into flames, and the aircraft plunged down – it was finished. Then I was out of ammo. Jaap Eden had gone. I couldn't see anything but enemy aeroplanes. There were none of ours any more.'

Having lost sight of Kiel, Eden damaged a Bf 110 and returned to Ypenburg, landing smack in the middle of a ground battle. His aircraft caught fire and Eden was captured by German paratroopers. Kiel wisely made for Ruigenhoek, an auxiliary airfield north of Leiden whose personnel were still in their beds when he and a few of his 2nd JaVA colleagues landed. 'Then we must bomb Berlin', shouted the local commander, other-worldly, upon learning the news. Kiel elected to refuel and depart, alone, to find assistance for his now malfunctioning guns. Nobody stopped him. Shortly after taking off he was attacked by five Bf 110s and wounded, his D.XXI spiralling down from 2500 ft and crashing in a German paratroop drop zone north of The Hague. Guus Kiel survived and eventually reached a hospital.

The Field Army 1st JaVA's third flight was comprised of Lt Droste and Sgt Aarts, who attacked a Ju 88 and a Bf 110, respectively. The Ju 88A of II./KG 30, which had been bombing a AAA battery, crashed just north of The Hague, its gunner having been killed. Droste and Aarts landed at Ockenburg shortly before this auxiliary airfield, too, was invaded by Gen Kurt Student's paratroops.

Ypenburg and Ockenburg were retaken by Dutch troops later in the day, the airborne assault against the Dutch seat of government, which did not come as a complete surprise, being a costly failure. Both airfields were littered with wrecked

Sgt Guus Kiel had a reputation for being both an able pilot and a bit of a daredevil. On 10 May he claimed a probable against a Ju 52/3m, but was subsequently shot down by five Bf 110s. Grounded by the war, he opened the *Flying Dutchman* pub on Amsterdam's Leidseplein, which became something of a resistance hotbed. Ironically, Kiel spent his youth in Germany, where he was 'infected by the flying bug' by none other than World War 1 ace Ernst Udet, whom he knew personally (*G Kiel*)

Guus Kiel survived the crash of his aircraft, No 216, in a German airborne drop zone near Wassenaar (*J van den Heuvel*)

Wachtmeester Jaap 'Jacky' van Zuijlen, who was killed in action as a 'White Mice' 1st JaVA pilot on 10 May, rode horses and drove armoured cars as well as flying aircraft. He served as an instructor on Koolhoven FK.51 intermediate trainers before receiving a D.XXI posting (*A Goossens*)

Ju 52/3ms, however, rendering the few surviving Field Army D.XXIs unusable. Only Lt Van der Vaart's machine was still airworthy at Schiphol. Three kills had been achieved by the pilots – the Bf 110s claimed by Aarts, Eden and Linzel must have been damaged aircraft, as II.ZG 1 reported no losses, although several *Zerstörer* limped home on one engine.

'WHITE MICE' 1st JaVA

De Kooy Naval Air Station near Den Helder was not initially attacked, and by 0359 hrs all 11 D.XXIs of the 'White Mice' 1st JaVA were airborne in four orderly flights. Columns of smoke over the airfields at Bergen and Texel Island confirmed the reality of war. Lt Frans Focquin de Grave's 'Kleuter' flight spotted five Bf 109s over Bergen and gave chase, but it could not get within effective range of the faster German fighters.

The 'Mina' flight of Lt Bob van der Stok and Lt Herman Doppenberg's 'Herman' flight went after a lone He 111 reconnaissance aircraft that flew south at 10,000 ft, and in doing so caught sight of some other German aircraft. When the four flights were called back to De Kooy, *Wachtmeester* (cavalry or artillery sergeant) Jaap van Zuijlen, who did not have a radio, did not follow Doppenberg and continued the chase south. 'Jacky' van Zuijlen was probably killed by an He 111 gunner, his D.XXI being seen to overfly the Hague battle zone in an incoherent manner before crashing in the coastal dunes.

Wachtmeester Willem Hateboer peeled off from 'Mina' flight north of Leiden to attack an aircraft 'packed with people', which 'tumbled down until it hit the dividing line of beach and sea'. Although his victim is reported to have been a Ju 88, Hateboer's account suggests a Ju 52/3m transport and, indeed, only Junkers trimotors came down on the beaches. Hateboer landed at Schiphol to refuel, before returning to De Kooy, where, meanwhile, the largest aerial battle of the Dutch campaign had been fought.

The returning 'White Mice' pilots could not prevent a strafing attack against De Kooy by two Bf 109s at 0430 hrs that killed an operator in the unit's radio truck. Doppenberg did escort in a diverting Fokker T.V bomber, however. With 'Kleuter' flight providing top cover, the other flights now came in to refuel.

At 0450 hrs, just as 'Kleuter' itself landed, nine Bf 109s attacked. Focquin de Grave turned his D.XXI around after landing and raced to take off again, barely missing Lt Jan Bosch's landing aircraft, which burst into flames after being targeted by the Bf 109s – its pilot escaped unhurt. Lt Henk van Overvest, the flight's other wingman, aborted his landing and zoomed up steeply. A ten-minute dogfight now ensued between the four D.XXI flights, now with two aircraft each, and the nine Bf 109Es of 5./JG 186 (a unit also known as 5.(J)/Tr.Gr.186, as it was once destined for service aboard the *Graf Zeppelin*, Germany's abortive aircraft carrier).

Bob van der Stok found himself in the thick of the action, as he later recalled;

Lt Jan Bosch stands by his burnt out D.XXI, No 241, after being caught by Bf 109s while landing at De Kooy (*T Postma*)

'They had already expended a fair amount of ammo on the ground targets, and had quite a long way to go home. This may have been why they seemed to hesitate when it came to attacking us. I saw four Messerschmitts with D.XXIs on their tails, and there was shooting. All over the place we saw German tracer bullets flashing through the sky. One Hun was already leaving a long white trail of petrol behind him. I think Doppenberg was flying alongside me, and just in front of us was a Messerschmitt in a slow turn. We opened fire simultaneously. Again, a white streak of petrol trailed behind the Hun aeroplane as it dashed away eastward.

'Barely was this done with when I saw an Me 109 [*sic*] coming straight towards me from the left. I banked my still-intact D.XXI into a hard left turn. I flew three complete circles with him until I finally got on his tail. The German pilot, realising the D.XXI could out-turn his Me 109, changed course towards the right and went into a dive. This was a serious error, as it placed him at exactly the right deflection angle for me to fire. This time I saw the white petrol plume and a black streak of oil, part of which even ended up on my windscreen. The Me 109 pulled up abruptly and then went into a spin.

'All over De Kooy I saw Me 109s and D.XXI fighters. Nearby there was another Me 109 with landing flaps deployed but wheels up. Much farther away there were two more Me 109s, one trailing a white smoke plume and the other apparently trying to escort it. On the horizon were two black dots heading east. I saw a pair of D.XXIs land and suddenly everything was quiet. Alongside me appeared "Spanky" van Overvest in a heavily damaged D.XXI full of bullet holes and his flaps half-extended. He gave me the thumbs-up and I gathered that he too had placed hits.'

Van Overvest, who landed a smoking aircraft, his face slightly wounded by the impact of a 20 mm shell in his cockpit, had indeed scored hits. His victim, Hauptmann Dietrich Robitzsch, belly-landed his aeroplane at De Kooy airfield, and on alighting inquired as to why the Dutch were putting up resistance. He spent the rest of the war as a PoW, as a shipload of captured Germans were despatched to Britain before Holland's surrender.

Herman Doppenberg had also shot down a Bf 109, which crashed in a polder southeast of Den Helder. Its pilot, Unteroffizier Rudolf, died of his wounds four days later. A damaged Bf 109 that made it to Borkum Island was shared by Focquin de Grave and Van der Stok. No further losses were reported by 5./JG 186, despite the usual overclaiming on both sides. The German pilots claimed four D.XXIs shot down, but only Lt Bosch's aircraft had been destroyed. The 'White Mice' 1st JaVA did well in this battle, demonstrating that the D.XXI, while inferior to the Bf 109, was no turkey.

Only two more sorties were flown over the next few hours, by Lts Van der Stok and Tuininga, while the groundcrew worked frantically to effect repairs. The unit received orders to leave De Kooy for Buiksloot, an auxiliary airfield in north Amsterdam, but before it could depart

The pilots of 'Kleuter' flight, photographed by Bob van der Stok on 10 May. Lt Henk van Overvest, on the left, had just scored his second kill, although he was slightly wounded in the face whilst doing so. Flight leader Lt Frans Focquin de Grave, who was the first to fire the D.XXI's guns in anger, in September 1939, shared a Bf 109 with van der Stok, and destroyed a Bf 110 the next day. On the right is Lt Jan Bosch, who flew a total of five sorties during the May war. He escaped to England and became a de Havilland Mosquito pilot (*T Postma*)

Lt Bram 'Bob' van der Stok was photographed with his own camera at De Kooy on 10 May 1940. He shared a Bf 109 with Frans Focquin de Grave that morning, and flew seven sorties during the May war. He reached England and subsequently claimed a Bf 109 shot down and three damaged as a Spitfire pilot with No 41 Sqn during 1942, but was shot down over France by Fw 190s on 12 April 1942. He successfully escaped from Stalag Luft III prison camp and arrived in Britain once more on 11 July 1944 (*D van Faassen*)

considerable damage was sustained in repeat attacks on the naval air station by the Luftwaffe at around 0800 hrs and again at noon. Two D.XXIs were destroyed on the ground and all of the others were damaged, two of them beyond speedy repair.

——— 2nd JaVA ———

At 0355 hrs Schiphol was attacked by Ju 88 and He 111 bombers of KG 4, and AAA opened up. The nine operational D.XXIs of the 2nd JaVA all got airborne, but the pilots were forced to engage the enemy individually, as did the Fokker T.V bombers that also took off – they had been engaged in neutrality enforcement patrols, and were therefore not in dispersed positions.

After the battle. Lt Herman Doppenberg, who was 6 ft 6 in tall, and Lt Henk van Overvest both destroyed a Bf 109 in the large dogfight over Den Helder on 10 May. Van Overvest also destroyed a He 111 in the run-up to the war. Following Holland's occupation he tried to join the RAF, but did not succeed in reaching Britain until late 1944 (*T Postma*)

The duty officer, Lt Sluijter, who had grabbed the nearest D.XXI, managed to shoot down a Ju 88, which crashed near Hoofddorp, killing the gunner. Sluijter then evaded to Ruigenhoek with the other pilots of his flight, Sgts Looijen and De Geus, the latter having attacked a He 111 and a Ju 88. Another pilot, Sgt Hein Bulten, was slightly wounded and landed his D.XXI in a field near Hoorn – it was eventually captured by the Germans. The unit's remaining five pilots returned to Schiphol between 0418 hrs and 0445 hrs. Lt Hans Plesman, who had been the last to take to the air, in Sluijter's aircraft, battled a formation of Bf 109s and landed in a bullet-riddled Fokker. The airport was still under attack, but the D.XXIs were serviced under the leadership of Lt Antoine Bodaan, who took off alone for a second sortie at 0448 hrs.

Pilots Plesman and Roos were sent to Ruigenhoek to join Lt Sluijter's flight. Now five D.XXIs strong, the latter took off for a fighter patrol over western Holland at 0730 hrs. Near Gouda, they fell upon a lone Ju 52/3m that had managed to take off from Ypenburg and was making for Germany, carrying the crew of a damaged Ju 52/3m and a wounded paratrooper. Sluijter was slightly wounded by the Ju 52/3m's dorsal gunner, but two of the transport's engines were set on fire by the Dutch pilots, Sgt De Geus inflicting substantial damage and Lt Hans Plesman delivering the final blow. Feldwebel Armbrust crash-landed his aircraft near Stolwijk, and all on board were taken prisoner by the Dutch.

Following this action Sgt Frans Looijen was missing – he had been caught by five Bf 109s of 3./JG 26 and shot down by *Staffelführer*, and future 57-victory ace, Oberleutnant Johannes Seifert. Looijen was killed as his D.XXI crashed into the Hollandse IJssel River. Two more sorties were flown by the 2nd JaVA later in the morning, Plesman and Roos strafing German aircraft on Katwijk beach and seeing some air combat.

All aircraft returned to Schiphol, where a remarkable figure had, meanwhile, reported to the unit – Carel Steensma, a KLM airline and former fighter pilot who had some limited D.XXI experience. He had

Scrambling from Schiphol, Lt Nicolaas Sluijter (or Sluyter) shot down a Ju 88 bomber on 10 May. Leading a five-aircraft mission later that same morning, he was wounded in the arm by a Ju 52/3m gunner but flew two more missions on 12 and 14 May. Sluijter later escaped to England and joined the RAF (*via F Gerdessen*)

been instructed to fly a KLM Douglas DC-3 to England, but the aircraft was damaged and he volunteered to fly D.XXIs 'for a couple of days'. Sgt Steensma was scheduled for the next assignment – a six-aircraft escort mission for three T.Vs. The target was Waalhaven, Rotterdam's airfield, which had also been taken by the German paratroopers.

A layer of clouds at 2000 ft offered some protection on the way in, but near Rotterdam the Dutch formation was intercepted by a gaggle of Bf 109s, several Luftwaffe units being involved in flying top cover for the German forces on the ground. Led by Lt Bodaan, the D.XXI pilots engaged the Messerschmitts, allowing the T.Vs to make a successful bombing run. Lt Henk Sitter, who had lost sight of his comrades in the clouds, followed the bombers, however, and strafed Ju 52/3ms on the airfield. He then saw six more Bf 109s going after the three T.Vs. Despite Sitter's best efforts (he claimed a Bf 109 shot down), both outer bombers were shot down in flames by the Messerschmitts of 1./JG 51 and eight Dutch airmen on board were killed.

Sergeant pilots of the 2nd JaVA at Eelde in March 1940. Frans Looijen, second from the right, was shot down by Bf 109s and killed on 10 May. Hein Bulten (in the leather jacket) was lightly wounded and Koos Roos (far right) badly wounded on that same day. Ben de Geus (left) flew eight combat sorties through to 14 May. Aircraft No 235 was Lt Hans Plesman's mount during the campaign (*via F Gerdessen*)

Meanwhile, in a confused dogfight against the other Bf 109 formation, the D.XXI flight leader, Bodaan, was shot down near Rhoon and killed – he was posthumously invested with the Military Order of William. Ben de Geus and Hans Plesman scored some hits against the Messerschmitts, as did volunteer pilot Steensma, who recalled;

'When I fired my four machine guns I jumped out of my skin. Tracer bullets flashed straight in front of me and I thought I was being shot at from behind. I had never fired tracer ammo in my life. I circled around briefly, and saw Me 109s at a higher altitude than my own. Me 109s to the left and to the right – a neat *Kette*, high above me. I remember my exact thoughts at that moment. "Look, that's a professional job". What I was doing myself appeared highly amateurish and awkward to me, and unreal in particular.'

Nonetheless, Steensma went on to shoot down two Bf 109s, or so he believed, and in classic fashion then forgot to 'check his six';

'Surprised at how quick and easy it was actually done, I climbed with my engine roaring to regain altitude, and was completely surprised by a crackling racket. Fire seemed to shoot between my legs, and I literally froze with fright. Looking inside the cockpit I saw that my dashboard was destroyed. Oil dripped on my feet, loose rags were dangling from the right wing and my right leg felt odd. I felt it and immediately had a bloody hand.'

A fire in his aircraft died spontaneously, and he was able to land at Schiphol without flaps or brakes. The heavily damaged D.XXI was a write-off, but Steensma was only lightly wounded, and even continued his voluntary service. The remaining four D.XXIs also found their way back into Schiphol.

In this battle 6./JG 27 claimed two D.XXIs destroyed without suffering any losses, the victory against Bodaan being credited to Lt Julius Neumann, *not* to future JG 3 ace Herbert Springer, as has been reported. Apparently, 8./JG 26 did also take part in this battle, and had two Bf 109s damaged, possibly by the D.XXI pilots, although none of their claims can be confirmed.

COMBINED JaVA

At 1400 hrs Air Defence headquarters ordered the 2nd JaVA to join the 'White Mice' 1st JaVA at Buiksloot, assembling the dozen or so surviving D.XXIs into a single unit. The surviving G.Is were being brought together at Schiphol. Buiksloot was just a small glider airfield on a wasteland near the NDSM shipyard in north Amsterdam, offering little cover or facilities. Its advantages were its proximity to the Fokker works, and the fact that the Germans seemed unaware of it.

At 1600 hrs on 10 May five 2nd JaVA aircraft and the single surviving Field Army 1st JaVA machine hopped over from Schiphol to Buiksloot, followed by a pair of patched-up D.XXIs from De Kooy in the evening. Three more repaired 'White Mice' aeroplanes arrived during the morning of 11 May, and one on 12 May. Added to the combined unit were five D.XVII biplane fighters from the advanced flying school on Texel Island, flown by novice pilots including Lt Jan Plesman, Hans Plesman's younger brother. Oddly, two serviceable D.XXIs and one G.I remained with the flying school, eventually to be destroyed or captured.

Luftwaffe activity over Holland decreased after the first day, but clearly the Germans had air superiority, and the Dutch fighters were generally tasked with escort missions flown at treetop height. For example, during the morning of 11 May, six D.XXIs escorted C.V biplanes on reconnaissance flights towards the east, with poor results, although the Luftwaffe was not encountered.

Later that day the two surviving T.V bombers flew two missions to Rotterdam but failed to take out their target – the bridges across the Nieuwe Maas River in central Rotterdam that had been captured by airborne troops. Escort each time was provided by a flight of three D.XXIs. The first formation returned safely to Schiphol and Buiksloot, but the second, in the early afternoon, was attacked by 12 Bf 110s after their bombing run. Two Dutch airmen were killed when one T.V was shot down by three of the I./ZG 1 heavy fighters, six of which went after the experienced D.XXI flight leader, Lt Frans Focquin de Grave.

In the ensuing dogfight he shot down a Bf 110C from 3./ZG I, which crashed near Gorinchem, badly wounding the pilot, Feldwebel Stadler. Focquin de Grave had, however, been wounded in the stomach, and he landed on the Hague–Utrecht highway, which had wisely been barricaded against possible Ju 52/3m landings. The D.XXI duly somersaulted onto its back, and as the Messerschmitts strafed his wrecked aircraft, the wounded pilot was able to take cover under a flyover, and survived.

The other three Bf 110s attacked the D.XXI of Sgt Koos Roos, who jettisoned his cockpit canopy as a precaution. The hood famously smashed into a DB 601 engine of a pursuing Messerschmitt. Roos escaped into a cloud, and on emerging he attacked another Bf 110, but

One of three D.XXI pilots killed in action during the May war, flight leader Lt Antoine Bodaan was shot down in a dogfight over Rotterdam by Leutnant Julius Neumann of 6./JG 27, who was flying a Bf 109. Bodaan was posthumously invested with the Military Order of William for his valour and leadership (*Leeuwarden Air Force Base*)

was then shot down – by Dutch AAA according to legend, but more likely by another Messerschmitt. Roos bailed out but was badly wounded, and his D.XXI crashed into the peaty soil near Nieuwkoop. The wreck was excavated in 1993 and is now displayed in the Crash Museum in Aalsmeerderbrug, near Schiphol.

Only the last remaining T.V and the D.XXI of Sgt Gé Burger returned from this mission. Focquin de Grave and Roos were unofficially credited with two Bf 110s each, and the downed T.V's tail gunner claimed a fifth. In fact, only Stadler's aircraft was destroyed, while another 3./ZG I Bf 110C returned to its base at Kirchhellen (Schwarze Heide) with a badly wounded gunner on board, the harm having been inflicted by either Focquin de Grave or Roos.

Discounting a short two-aircraft patrol later in the afternoon, the next D.XXI action occurred early the following day, Whit Sunday, when two three-aircraft flights set out to escort some C.Vs. Volunteer pilot Sgt Steensma took off prematurely, and when landing again his undercarriage ran into a hole in the field and the aircraft somersaulted. Brave Carel Steensma was now finally hospitalised, his D.XXI another write-off. Lts Tuininga and Sgt De Geus escorted two C.Vs on a reconnaissance mission towards the east. Although Bf 109s were seen, they disappeared, perhaps low on fuel. A German reconnaissance aircraft was reportedly attacked over Arnhem by Ben de Geus, the engine of his patched-up 'White Mice' D.XXI momentarily cutting in the process. Led by Lt Van Overvest, the other flight escorted four C.Vs, two of which bombed alleged positions of airborne troops north of Rotterdam.

During the afternoon of the 12th Lt Sluijter led six D.XXIs on another mission to Rotterdam, escorting four C.Xs. Three D.XXIs and two of the biplanes attacked the car park of the Feyenoord Football Stadium, which the Germans supposedly intended to use as an airstrip. The other five Fokkers bombed and strafed Waalhaven airfield. Bob van der Stok participated in this attack, later noting, 'With everything we had – D.XXIs with bullet holes, no canopies and leaking brake systems – we attacked with the sun at our backs'.

Some D.XXIs did indeed now fly without canopies, either as a result of combat damage or because the pilot got a better view without one. It was also easier to bail out of the fighter if there was no canopy to jettison. All ten aircraft returned safely from this mission.

12 May also saw D.XXI pilot *Wachtmeester* Hateboer ordered to escort the last T.V bomber on a dubious mission towards the north, where the strong fortress at the eastern end of the Afsluitdijk Dam was not actually under serious attack. The pilots wisely turned back.

Although Rotterdam remained the focal point of the German invasion, the Wehrmacht was by now also attacking the main defensive line in the central Netherlands, the Grebbe Line. A support mission by four C.Vs and one C.X received an escort of D.XVII biplanes on their one and only combat assignment, the veteran fighters being led by 19-year-old rookie pilot Lt Stuy. Although the Luftwaffe was not encountered, several of the D.XVIIs were damaged in takeoff and landing accidents.

After a few hours of sleep in the shipyard workers' society building, groundcrew and pilots of the combined JaVA woke up early on 13 May for another mission to the Grebbe Line. At 0347 hrs, five C.X biplanes took off from their Bergen base and flew to Buiksloot to pick up their five D.XXI escorts, led by Lt Doppenberg, 11 minutes later – a sixth D.XXI was grounded by an hydraulic leak. The biplanes dropped their 50 kg bombs on German artillery positions near Wageningen and the aircraft strafed enemy troops. Despite suffering some damage from ground fire, all returned safely. This mission was considered successful, and was repeated around noon. Again, the four C.Xs and five D.XXIs all made it back to base, but ever more combat damage was being accumulated by the Fokker fighters.

The Grebbe Line fell that day, and after nightfall the Dutch Field Army began its precarious retreat to the old Water Line, further west. All the remaining fighters were ordered to fly top cover for the retreat from dawn. The first flight of five D.XXIs, led by Lt Tuininga, took off as morning fog cleared. The enemy was not encountered, but Lt Sitter suffered an engine failure and landed in a field west of Utrecht, where his aircraft was later burned by the Dutch. The others landed at Schiphol, to where the D.XXI squadron had been moved because of fears of a German landing, however unlikely, to the north of Amsterdam. Eight D.XXIs were reported combat ready at 1015 hrs, and a final mission was completed by five D.XXIs flown by Lts Sluijter, Bik, Plesman, Van der Vaart and Van der Stok.

The Dutch defeat seemed inevitable, but still not imminent, and early that afternoon the Luftwaffe bombed the centre of Rotterdam, where the north bank of the Nieuwe Maas was still held by Dutch marines. Although the local German commander had requested a tactical bombardment, it was stepped up to a terror raid by a whole *Gruppe* of He 111s, killing more than 800 people. The remaining few Dutch fighter aircraft were clearly powerless. Leaflets threatened Utrecht with a similar fate, and at 1650 hrs the Dutch surrendered, except in Zeeland province.

At Schiphol the nine serviceable D.XXIs were destroyed by the Dutch themselves. Capt Schmidt Crans holed the fuel tanks with his pistol and then a match was put to them. Some nine other D.XXIs, either stranded or unserviceable, were captured by the Germans, and at least two saw service with the Luftwaffe's flying instructor school at Brandenburg-Briest.

Ten credible kills were achieved by the D.XXI pilots, all but one on the first day, comprising three Bf 109s, one Bf 110, one Do 17, three Ju 52/3ms and two Ju 88s. Henk van Overvest added one victory to his He 111 kill of 1939, and 1.5 kills can be credited to Frans Focquin de Grave.

As the Occupation began, quite a few of the D.XXI pilots tried to reach Britain. Not all attempts were successful – Boy Ruijs de Perez and Carel Steensma were arrested and tortured as resistance fighters, Ruijs de Perez being shot. Pilots Bosch, Linzel, Sipkes, Sluijter (or Sluyter), Steen and Van der Stok, as well as Fokker pilot Hidde Leegstra, all became RAF pilots. Govert Steen was killed in a Spitfire near Le Havre in 1942, while Bob van der Stok was also shot down over France and became famous through successfully escaping from Stalag Luft III. None of the D.XXI pilots became aces. Indeed, the Dutch did not produce any aces whatsoever, unless V1 'kills' are counted.

OBSOLESCENCE

I n the spring of 1939 Finland had begun to try and find a successor for the Fokker D.XXIs then in service. The tense political situation in Europe did not favour such attempts, and when Germany suddenly attacked Poland on 1 September 1939, almost all channels of supply dried up. Realising that no new foreign fighters would be available any time soon, the *Ilmavoimat*, on 9 September, placed an order with the State Aircraft Factory for 50 licence-built D.XXIs.

Since all of the locally licence-built Bristol Mercury engines were destined for the Bristol Blenheim bombers then also being built under licence, Finland opted to replace the D.XXI's original powerplant with the American Pratt & Whitney R-1535 Twin Wasp Junior engine as it was in the same power category. The State Aircraft Factory asked Fokker to design the installation, which was to be the last major modification made to the D.XXI by the Dutch manufacturer.

However, the order did not proceed, as on 30 November 1939 the Soviet Union attacked Finland and the matter was shelved simply because the whole capacity of the State Aircraft Factory was used to return damaged combat aircraft to airworthiness.

Following the implementation of the peace treaty that ended the Winter War things returned to normal in Finland, but only for a short while. On 9 April 1940, only four weeks after the fighting with the USSR has ceased, Germany invaded Denmark and Norway. The former fell in just two days, but owing to Norway's rather more challenging geography it took the Germans two months to gain control of the whole country.

The occupation of much of Scandinavia by the Germans had an adverse effect on Finland. The vital war supplies it had been receiving from Britain and France had previously been shipped or flown to Norway and then sent on to Finland via Sweden. This route was now cut off. Finland had just one point of access remaining – the port of Petsamo, in the Arctic Sea. It would subsequently handle all exports and imports, apart from those to and from Germany, for a year. It was also the route by which R-1535 engines arrived to power newly-built D.XXIs.

When the Finns resurrected the Twin Wasp programme, the Fokker factory was no longer able to offer assistance as the Netherlands had been invaded by Germany. The original design needed changing so that the R-1535 could be fitted to the airframe, and the State Aircraft Factory duly designed the tools to manufacture new engine bearers, in addition to the cowlings, cooling gills and intakes. The cockpit was

The licence-built IV series D.XXIs were powered by 825 hp Pratt & Whitney R-1535 Twin Wasp Junior radial engines. One of the first, FR-129, is seen here at the Air Depot at Kuorevesi. On 30 March 1941 it was handed over to LLv 30 and assigned to the 2nd Flight leader 1Lt Veikko Karu, the Continuation War's top-scoring D.XXI pilot (*Finnish Air Force Museum*)

given a longer rear-view canopy, the electrical systems were redesigned and all armament was transferred to the wings.

Finnish-built Mercury-powered D.XXIs had suffered from vibration in the tail unit, most noticeably in the rudder. Starting from early 1940, reinforcement of the tail was carried out during major overhauls. The rudder was fitted with a third hinge and a mass balance replaced the aerodynamic balance. The tailplane was now built with two spars supported by a V-strut instead of a single strut. In addition, the fuel and oil tanks were rubber coated and the pilot's seat was fitted with armour plating. All of these improvements were incorporated into the Twin Wasp-powered D.XXI.

The prototype, FR-118, was first flown on 29 October 1940 by 1Lt Erkki Itävuori, an experienced test pilot who had also downed four Soviet bombers whilst defending the State Aircraft Factory during the Winter War. The prototype's flying characteristics, though slightly inferior to those of the standard Mercury-powered D.XXI, were acceptable, especially as there were no alternatives available.

Series production started in January 1941, and within six months all 50 had been built – just in time for the Continuation War. One more major modification was introduced after two months of combat experience. Twin Wasp-powered D.XXIs had some stalling problems, and these were corrected by fitting anti-stall slots in the wingtips, similar to those seen in the Soviet Lavochkin LaGG-3 fighter or American Douglas SBD Dauntless dive-bomber. These also improved the fighter's turning characteristics and gave better control at slow speed when landing.

HOME DEFENCE

During the Winter War the aid from Britain and France, in addition to purchases from the USA and Italy, built the strength of LeR 2 up to 100 aircraft. The 50 D.XXIs on order from the factory would dramatically increase this figure. Therefore, another fighter regiment, LeR 3, was established on 29 March 1940. Like its sister unit, it would consist of three squadrons. LLv 30 would receive the new Wasp-powered D.XXIs, while LLv 32 would get the surviving Mercury-engined Fokker fighters. The third squadron, LLv 34, was intended to be equipped with French Caudron CR.714 fighters, but as only six arrived from France, it instead became an advanced training outfit with a mixed fleet of biplanes.

Operation *Barbarossa*, the German invasion of the Soviet Union (decided upon in December 1940), was planned to begin after the spring thaw season. However, the German occupation of Yugoslavia and the Balkans saw *Barbarossa* postponed until 22 June 1941. By this time the Third Reich had used various methods to persuade other countries that shared a border with the Soviet Union, or were geographically close to it, such as Hungary, Rumania, Bulgaria and Finland, to side with Germany. *Barbarossa* was revealed to the Finnish military leadership only four weeks before its launch. Armed with this information, the Finns mobilised for war on 17 June, five days before *Barbarossa* was launched.

Large numbers of German aircraft were moved to airfields in southern Finland just before the offensive commenced, these machines carrying out reconnaissance and channel mining missions. Soviet intelligence soon detected the presence of Luftwaffe aircraft at Finnish bases, and it assumed that these airfields would also be used by German bombers for raids on nearby Leningrad. The VVS therefore decided to attack these airfields, drawing up a plan for a six-day bombing offensive. For this purpose the VVS (Leningrad Military District, parts of Baltic Military District, Northern Fleet and Baltic Fleet) had at their disposal, from the Arctic Sea to the Baltic Sea, 2503 warplanes, of which 933 were bombers and 1327 fighters. In addition, 202 long-range bombers were in the rear.

FR-113 of 2/LLv 32, lightly camouflaged at Hyvinkää on the opening day of the Continuation War, 25 June 1941, was routinely flown by the flight's deputy leader, 1Lt Lauri Bremer. During the first weeks of the Continuation War LLv 32 flew numerous combat air patrols over southern Finland (*A Bremer*)

The operational borderline between Germany and Finland observed by the VVS ran from east to west through Oulu, Kajaani and Belomorsk. South of this theoretical line on a map, half of the Soviet bomber force could be directed against Finland.

Soviet air raids on Finland began early in the morning of 25 June, a full 72 hours after the launching of *Barbarossa*. During the course of the day the communists generated 263 bomber and 224 fighter sorties against several locations in southern and southwestern Finland, including airfields and purely civilian targets. After these raids the Finnish parliament concluded that same day that a state of war existed between Finland and the Soviet Union. The Continuation War had begun.

The D.XXIs of LeR 3 were assigned the mission of home defence, and the regiment's order of battle on 25 June 1941 was as follows;

LeR 3
Regimental Commander, Lt Col E Nuotio, with HQ at Pori

LLv 30
Commander, Capt L Bremer, with HQ at Pori
– 1st Flight, Capt H Kalaja at Hollola with five Hurricanes
– 2nd Flight, 1Lt V Karu at Pori with 12 Wasp-D.XXIs
– 3rd Flight, 1Lt E Ilveskorpi at Turku with six Wasp-D.XXIs

LLv 32
Commander, Capt E Heinilä, with HQ at Hyvinkää
– 1st Flight, Capt P Berg at Hyvinkää with six Mercury-D.XXIs
– 2nd Flight, Capt K Lahtela at Hyvinkää with six Mercury-D.XXIs

LeR 3 was specifically tasked with protecting Finnish troop mobilisation from Soviet aerial attacks, as well as providing fighter cover for industrial plants in Lahti, Helsinki, Tammisaari and Turku. The latter town also boasted Finland's most important port, and LeR 3 was given the job of preventing it from being bombed. The regiment was also to provide fighter cover for vessels sailing in the Turku archipelago. Additionally, LLv 32 was specifically tasked with protecting the main railway line that ran north from Helsinki.

Observers in Turku initially spotted Soviet bomber formations entering the airspace of southern Finland at 0600 hours on 25 June. More aircraft were seen throughout the morning and well into the afternoon. One of the first units to encounter the bombers was LLv 32, based at Hyvinkää. 1Lt Veikko Evinen had led six D.XXIs from the 1st Flight aloft shortly before 0800 hrs, and minutes later he observed DB-3s returning south via Helsinki. Evinen shot down two of them, as he stated in his combat report;

Reconnaissance aeroplane FR-114 of 2/LLv 12 on the airfield at Mantsi, on the shoreline of Lake Ladoga, in August 1941. A few weeks earlier 1Lt Veikko Evinen of 1/LLv 32 had claimed the first Fokker kills of the Continuation War with the aircraft in this same guise (*Finnish Air Force Museum*)

'0800-0810 hrs. I engaged a nine-aircraft DB formation at 4000 metres [13,000 ft] flying eastwards. I fired at the aircraft flying a little behind the others on the right flank and saw its starboard engine burst into flames. The aircraft then went into a dive, so I began to fire at a second DB on the left flank of the formation, and managed to set its port engine aflame. The formation was then about ten kilometres [six miles] east of Helsinki, flying southwards. The first aircraft crashed about two kilometres [one mile] east of Malmi Airport and the second in the sea southeast of the bay of Puotinkylä. A large hole in the rear fuselage of my aircraft was probably caused by friendly flak. There was also a bullet mark in the propeller. I was flying aircraft FR-116.'

A tally of 26 Soviet bombers destroyed (23 later admitted by the communists) was not a bad start for the Continuation War, but the raids had exposed large gaps in the air surveillance network and fighter control system. Although 121 fighters were ready for interception, only a fifth of them could be directed to deal with the enemy. The weak spots were detected and filled, mainly by newer frontline fighters such as the Brewster Buffalo, Morane-Saulnier MS.406, Fiat G.50 and Curtiss Hawk.

The Soviet bombing offensive lasted six days, during which Finnish (and German) airfields were attacked on 39 occasions by a total of 992 aircraft, whose crews claimed 130 aircraft had been destroyed on the ground or in the air. In reality the Luftwaffe suffered no losses, since it had already moved its units eastward to captured Soviet airfields. Losses for the *Ilmavoimat* amounted to two slightly damaged aircraft. On the other hand the Finnish fighter pilots claimed to have shot down 34 Russian bombers during the same period.

Within a week of the Continuation War commencing, most VVS units originally in the Finnish sector of the front had been withdrawn to repel the German invasion further south. On the ground, 23rd Army on the Karelian Isthmus and 7th Army north of Lake Ladoga and up to Uhtua were

The mount of LLv 32 commander Capt Erkki Heinilä, FR-109 is seen at Utti in early July 1941. Heinilä shared in the destruction of a DB-3M bomber with Cpl Mauno Kirjonen on 8 July 1941. The 'White X' adorning FR-109's rudder was Heinilä's personal marking (*Finnish Aviation Museum*)

responsible for repelling any invasion attempted by the Finns. VVS units supporting 23rd Army consisted of 5th SAD (*Smeshannaya Aviatsionnaya Diviziya* – Composite Aviation Division), which controlled 7th and 153rd IAPs and 65th and 235th ShAPs (*Shturmovoy Aviatsionnaya Polk* – Ground attack Aviation Regiment), while 7th Army was assigned 55th SAD, consisting of 72nd SBAP and 155th, 179th, 197th and 415th IAPs. The number of combat aircraft mustered by these two air divisions did not exceed 300. Additionally, the Baltic Fleet Air Forces left 30 fighters and about 50 seaplanes at various bases in the Gulf of Finland.

Capt Paavo Berg, leader of 1/LLv 32, taxied into a car used by war correspondents at Utti on 9 July 1941. Not wanting to walk, the reporters had driven too far out onto the active airfield. Berg was already a Gladiator ace from the Winter War, and he added more victories with the Hawk 75A to finish with a total of 10.5 kills (*SA-kuva*)

SOUTHERN FINLAND

By 3 July LeR 3 was also tasked with protecting the field army southwest of the River Vuoksi and the industrial areas at Vuoksenlaakso. LLv 32 was transferred closer to the front at Utti in order to perform these missions more effectively. At the same time the main component of LLv 30 flew to Hyvinkää, from where it was to protect southern and southwestern Finland. The most visible elements of its mission were the interception of enemy aircraft over the Gulf of Finland and strafing attacks on coastal patrol boats of the Soviet navy.

On 6 July 3/LLv 30 drew first blood in the southern sector when a *swarm* led by 1Lt Martti Kalima scrambled at dawn and claimed the unit's first aerial victory in the form of a lone SB bomber of 117th RAE (*Razvedyvatel'nyy Aviatsionnyy Eskadrilya* – Reconnaissance Aviation Squadron) on a reconnaissance mission to the Turku area.

On 14 July LLv 30 became the only fighter squadron flying D.XXIs when LLv 32 exchanged its Fokkers for Curtiss Hawks. By this point the D.XXIs of the latter unit had shot down five Soviet bombers.

Eight days later 3/LLv 30, which had remained in the defence of

Wasp-powered D.XXI FR-160 of 3/LLv 32 at Vesivehmaa in early July 1941. 'Yellow 1' was assigned to flight leader and future ace 1Lt Aulis Bremer, who claimed all of his 7.5 kills flying the Hawk 75A (*A Bremer*)

southwestern Finland, engaged a fighter *swarm* north of Turku airfield. Leading the Finnish aircraft was 1Lt Martti Kalima, who claimed two Soviet machines destroyed;

'North of the airfield we took a four-aeroplane (two I-16s and two I-153s) patrol by surprise. One of the I-153s was lagging behind, and we attacked this machine from above and behind. I fired off a burst from a long distance, after which we started to chase the Polikarpovs. North of Pensari Island, just when we were about to come within effective firing

range of the enemy fighters, five I-153s and four I-16s appeared on the scene from south of the island. We could not avoid this encounter, which commenced at an altitude of less than 100 metres [330 ft].

'At one stage an I-16 had managed to get behind one of our machines. I shot at it in a bank from a distance of 50 metres [165 ft] and the fighter flipped over into a vertical dive and fell in the sea. During the combat all four aircraft in our patrol had to fire at the enemy fighters. We saw at least four of them break off the combat and head south. 2Lt Salomaa and I fired at one I-153, which went into a dive and crashed on Pensari Island, starting a large fire.

'The Russians avoided coming down to fight us at low level, which in turn meant that our best evasive manoeuvre when we were under attack was a fast horizontal banking turn just above the water.

'The antenna was shot off my aeroplane, FR-148, and a bullet passed through the main spar of the port wing, the aileron actuator and the wing trailing edge. There were five hits in the wingtip and my starboard tyre was punctured, although I landed without any problem.'

On 3 August three D.XXIs from 3/LLv 30 were scrambled from Turku to intercept approaching SB bombers, as SSgt Pentti Rekola recalled;

'Shortly after taking off at 1540 hrs I observed three enemy SB bombers flying westwards at about 4000 metres [13,000 ft] between the clouds east of Korppoo. I was then at about 3000 metres [10,000 ft], so I immediately began to climb hard towards them. When I got to within 800 metres [2640 ft] of the SBs at their altitude, a single SB bomber turned south and flew in the direction of the sea. The remaining two continued westward, and I went after them.

'When I got to within about 400 metres [1320 ft] of them they began to bank and changed course to the south. The fuselage gunner of the

Groundcrew attempt to hand-crank FR-125 of 2/LLv 30 into life at Hyvinkää on 9 July 1941, with 2Lt Oiva Louko watching on from the cockpit. The D.XXI's prominent undercarriage spats provided a suitable canvas for various styles of camouflage (*SA-kuva*)

aeroplane on the right started shooting at me, but I did not see the one on the left fire. I chose the right one as my target. Approaching to within 100 metres [330 ft] of the SB, I opened fire at the gunner, who slumped back into the fuselage and left his weapon hanging free in the turret. I then closed to within 50 metres [165 ft] of the SB and targeted both of its engines in turn. They began to smoke heavily and the starboard one caught fire. The aircraft then went into a 40-degree dive. I thought this one was done for, so I went after the other SB. The latter machine had by then raced off into the clouds and I did not see it again. My aeroplane was FR-150.'

──── GULF OF FINLAND ────

2/LLv 30 had enjoyed success whilst patrolling over the Gulf of Finland, shooting down a pair of Beriev MBR-2 flying boats of 15th AP KBF (*Aviatsionnyy Polk Krasnoznamyonnyy Baltiyskiy Flot* – Aviation Regiment of the Red Banner Baltic Fleet) on 8, 15 and 19 July. On the first occasion future D.XXI ranking ace 1Lt Veikko Karu claimed his first Continuation War victory to add to the three he had claimed during the Winter War.

For the Baltic Fleet Air Forces 5 August was a costly day. Pairs of D.XXIs from 2/LLv 30 flew several combat air patrols, and the Russians lost a total of five MBRs over the Gulf of Finland in three encounters. 2Lt Oiva Louko claimed 1.5 flying boats, as he noted in his combat report;

'I observed the enemy flying boats at 1040 hrs and chased after them. After they had spotted us they turned to evade in the direction of Estonia. I soon caught them and attacked the rearmost aircraft with Sgt Tirkkonen. I fired a long burst into the hull and engine from behind, and the flying boat caught fire. At the same time Sgt Tirkkonen shot at its port wing, which also burst into flames. The aeroplane crashed in the sea, still burning. I then went after the other machine. I soon caught up with it, and fired my first burst at the fuselage turret gunner, who instantly stopped firing. I then closed to within 30 metres [33 yd] of the flying boat and shot at its engine, which caught fire. The aircraft crashed into the sea and was burning when I left it. The first flying boat had sunk by then. My aeroplane was FR-127.'

These MBRs had come from three different units, namely 15th AP, 44th OAE (*Otdel'naya Aviatsionnyy Eskadrilya* – Independent Aviation Squadron) and 58th OAE, all of which belonged to Baltic Fleet Air Forces.

Its engine now running smoothly, FR-125 commences its takeoff run from Hyvinkää on 9 July 1941. This machine was assigned to 2Lt Ture Mattila, who had used it to shoot down an MBR-2 flying boat the day before this photograph was taken. Aircraft from this flight had prominent red and yellow tail numbers (*SA-kuva*)

On 5 August 1941 these men shot down four Baltic Fleet MBR-2 flying boats. They are, from left to right, Sgt Aaro Nuorala, 1Lt Teuvo Ruohola, an unnamed armourer, 2Lt Oiva Louko and Sgt Aarne Tirkkonen. Behind them is Ruohola's aeroplane, FR-119 (*Finnish Air Force Museum*)

Below right
D.XXIs of 2/LLv 30 sit on the grass at Hyvinkää between missions in late July 1941. They are, from right to left, FR-124, FR-122, FR-123 and FR-129. The nearest fighter was flown by the flight deputy leader, 1Lt Veikko Sauru. This flight had up to 25 aircraft on strength, which it used to effectively harass the Baltic Fleet's shipping and air forces (*T Mattila*)

Below
Photographed at Suulajärvi on 1 November 1941, FR-129 returned to base with a hole in its cowling after being struck by anti-aircraft fire. This machine was assigned to 2/LLv 30 leader Capt Veikko Karu. Twelve months later he was awarded the Mannerheim Cross for achievements against the Baltic Fleet shipping and air forces (*A Bremer*)

On 25 August Capt Veikko Karu and his wingman from 2/LLv 30 attacked two MBRs (which they misidentified as ARK flying boats) from 58th OAE near Pien-Tytärsaari, in the eastern Gulf of Finland, destroying them both. Karu described his victories in this manner;

'When I was on a combat air patrol south of Pien-Tytärsaari I observed two enemy aeroplanes at 1335 hrs. I signalled my wingman (2Lt Mattila) and began a pursuit. I caught the enemy machines, which had descended to the surface of the water, in just about five minutes. I directed my attack against the starboard aeroplane from straight behind. I shot at the engine and port wing root. When I got behind the aircraft's tail I observed a puff of smoke from its engine and received a shower of fuel on my windscreen. At the same time my machine guns jammed. I pulled up to the right and began making charging attempts from further off. When pulling up I looked over at my wingman, whom I saw pull up steeply to the left behind the other aircraft and then head north. I understood that he had had to abandon the fight for some reason [2Lt Mattila had been wounded by return fire].

'After getting my starboard guns to work again, I saw that the flying boats had continued to head south, the starboard one smoking slightly. I attacked this aircraft from the side, but because my shooting seemed to have no effect, and I received strong counter fire, I positioned myself directly behind its tail for my next attack. I shot a burst from a very short distance into the engine, whereupon it and the port wing caught fire. Immediately after this I shot a burst into the cockpit, and the aeroplane crashed in the sea ahead of me.

'I moved in behind the other aircraft and fired a long burst into its engine from very close range. The shooting appeared to have no effect at first, even though the bullets hit the target. All of a sudden the enemy machine burst into flames, and I almost collided with it. As I pulled over the flying boat my aircraft was flipped to the port side by a huge shockwave. After levelling off, I saw only debris on the surface of the sea, and further back behind me a black column of smoke was rising from the previous aircraft, which I saw in the water on my return flight to the north of Suursaari. I did not see either enemy aircraft make any evasive manoeuvres other than a couple of shallow banking turns. I used about 500 rounds, and there were 27 holes in my own aircraft, FR-129.'

Prior to this encounter Karu had scored 4.5 victories, so the two flying boats elevated him to ace status. He would ultimately be the only all-Fokker ace of the Continuation War.

On 1 September LLv 30 was given the job of protecting Kouvola, Kotka, Viipuri and Ylävuoksi, as well as Helsinki, Tammisaari and Turku on occasion. The unit was also ordered to transfer to Utti the following day.

Top right
Capt Veikko Karu, the leader of 2/LLv 30, with his groundcrew in front of FR-129 in September 1941. Tactical number 1 was usually applied to the flight leader's aeroplane. Karu's personal emblem on the fin was a devil chasing an I-16 fighter (*V Karu*)

Top left
The other side of FR-129's tail. The five victory bars indicate that this photograph was taken in early April 1942. The red and yellow number 1 on the rudder is barely discernible (*V Karu*)

Assigned to the deputy leader of 3/LLv 30, 1Lt Martti Kalima, FR-148 is seen after a successful forced landing in a field at Kuusio, in southern Finland, on 4 August 1941 by Cpl Urho Lehto (*via Seabird Publishing*)

By this point in the conflict Finnish troops on the Karelian Isthmus had reached the outer defensive lines of Leningrad, where Marshal Carl Mannerheim, commander-in-chief of the army, halted the offensive. The frontline was fixed along the Rajajoki-Valkeasaari-Lempaala-Tappari line.

LLv 30 subsequently experienced a six-week lull in action, after which the unit primarily strafed enemy vessels sailing in the Gulf of Finland. For example, on 17 October, while on a combat air patrol, Capt Veikko Karu's six-aircraft formation from 2/LLv 30 spotted a coastal freighter and sank it near Södeskär. On a later mission that same day Karu and his wingman set fire to a motor torpedo boat on the south side of Suursaari.

D.XXI FR-157 was assigned to the CO of LLv 30, Maj Lauri Bremer, at Utti in September 1941. While the CO of sister squadron LLv 32 had an 'X' on his Fokker (FR-109), Bremer chose an ace of hearts playing card, as the Finnish word for 'hearts' was his wife's name (*SA-kuva*)

On 29 October Capt Karu and his wingman undertook a reconnaissance mission to Seivästö, where they started a fire aboard a transport vessel and caused a 'guard ship to emit smoke'. Another 'guard ship' was set alight later in the patrol. Later that day in a sweep off Harjavalta, Karu's six-aircraft flight fired at a motor torpedo boat, which exploded east of Krasnaya Gorka.

On 1 November Capt Karu's six-strong flight fired at a tug and two 'guard boats' south of Koivisto. The tug caught fire and the 'guard boats' began to drift out of control. In the afternoon the same detachment observed three motor torpedo boats near Seiskari and set them alight – all three of them eventually blew up.

After Soviet forces had withdrawn into the shelter of the fortress of Kronstadt, on the outskirts of Leningrad, the airspace over the Gulf of Finland fell rather quiet. The last encounter of 1941 occurred on 17 December when 2/LLv 30, led by Capt Veikko Karu, engaged an MBR flying boat of 44th OAE KBF and its three I-153 escorts in the vicinity of Narvi lighthouse. Four D.XXIs attacked the escort fighters, which fled. Two Fokkers then shot down the flying boat.

The winter months were peaceful, but when spring approached Soviet forces again became active. On 14 March 1942 Capt Veikko Karu led five D.XXIs of 2/LLv 30 on a combat air patrol between Lavansaari and Rajajoki. Near Peninsaari they engaged a solitary MBR-2 flying boat of 15th AP KBF and shot it down.

Five days later the Finns decided to take back the island of Suursaari (Gogland), in the Gulf of Finland east of Helsinki, by advancing across the ice. Detachment Pajari was formed expressly for this purpose, and LeRs 3 and 4, LLv 6, 3/LLv 24 and an ambulance/liaison flight were ordered to support the operation – a total of 57 aircraft.

On 26 March LLv 30 flew 77 escort sorties, the unit having previously been involved in

The commander of LLv 30, Maj Lauri Bremer, poses in front of his machine, FR-157, at Utti on 13 November 1941. The kill marking on the rudder dates back to 6 August 1941, when 2Lt Ture Mattila, flying this machine, shared in the destruction of an MBR-2 flying boat with 1Lt Veikko Karu, who was flying FR-129 (*SA-kuva*)

Pilot 1Lt Teuvo Ruohola of 2/LLv 30 displays his achievements to war correspondent Pärttyli Virkki at Suulajärvi on 20 November 1941. The tallies on the tail of FR-119 record two aerial victories and three vessel sinkings (*SA-kuva*)

2Lt Ture Mattila in front of FR-125 at Utti on 13 November 1941. This photograph was taken at the end of a month's tour with the 1st Flight of 1/LLv 30, whose aircraft had white tactical numbers. Mattila's final score was 5.5 aerial victories (*SA-kuva*)

Pilots of 2/LLv 30 at Suulajärvi on 26 January 1942. They are, from left to right, flight leader Capt Veikko Karu, deputy leader 1Lt Veikko Sauru, Sgt Helge Krohn, 2Lt Reino Linko, Sgt Pentti Väisänen and 2Lt Tauno Saalasti (*SA-kuva*)

escorting troop transports that were taking troops to the Kotka-Hamina area prior to the launching of the offensive. From the 26th LLv 30's task was specified as 'the protection of the offensive of Battle Unit Pajari for the occupation of Suursaari'. The 1st and 2nd Flights duly deployed to an ice base at Lupinlahti, near Hamina, from where they operated for the next four days. The invasion began on the evening of 26 March.

The next day Capt Antti Naakka's six D.XXIs from 1/LLv 30 jointly flew a combat air patrol with a *swarm* of Curtiss Hawks from LLv 32 to Suursaari, where they engaged a mixed formation of VVS fighters. One I-153 was sent down and two more were damaged. An hour later Capt Veikko Karu of 2/LLv 30 was patrolling in the same area and he downed an I-153 from the same formation.

At dawn on 28 March it was 2/LLv 30's turn to fly a combat air patrol to Suursaari, and Capt Veikko Karu's seven Fokkers engaged a formation of about 20 fighters flying in two groups. During a ten-minute turning fight the Finns sent down three aircraft, after which the enemy fighters began to break off combat. The Fokkers briefly gave chase, but the VVS machines were too quick for them. Two of the three Polikarpovs downed by the flight were claimed by 1Lt Veikko Sauru, who reported;

'We engaged enemy fighters between 0545 hrs and 0610 hrs at an altitude of 1500-1000 metres [4900-3300 ft]. Having observed the enemy formation, I attacked those aircraft flying at the lowest height. During my climbing approach I reached the same altitude as a formation of six I-153s. Turning into one of them, I opened fire and saw smoke begin to trail from the aircraft. 2Lt Helle stayed on the tail of the aeroplane while I performed a head-on attack on a second I-153. I avoided colliding with the "Chaika" by pulling up and over it at the very last moment. 2Lt Mattila and Sgt Krohn, who observed my attack, saw the I-153 enter a spin and hit the deck. I fired at a few other I-153s and one I-16. I was flying aeroplane FR-124.'

28 March also saw Finnish troops seize Suursaari from the Red Army.

On 4 April Capt Antti Naakka's eight D.XXIs of 1/LLv 30 scattered a 100-man communist detachment heading from Tytärsaari to Lavansaari, and 1Lt Veikko Sauru's five fighters from 2/LLv 30 strafed a company on the ice between Seiskari and Harjavalta. Later that day the

LLv 30's CO Maj Lauri Bremer flew FR-157 (marked with his playing card emblem), which is seen on the ice at Lupinlahti, near Hamina, in mid-March 1942. Just before the Suursaari invasion on the 24th of that month, the aeroplane turned over on its back while landing at Suur-Merijoki (*A Bremer*)

same Sauru formation was attacked by a dozen 'Chaikas' during another mission to Seiskari, the Finns claiming two enemy fighters destroyed. One of the pilots to make a claim was Sgt Otto Karme, who recalled;

'Our five-aeroplane formation, led by 1Lt Sauru, was heading west towards Seiskari at 1605 hrs at an altitude of 500 m [1640 ft] when we spotted a six-aircraft enemy formation flying directly towards us. We did not see another six-aeroplane formation flying above them. The observed enemy fighters were I-153s, and we attacked them head-on from slightly below. I saw my burst of fire hit the engine of an I-153, but I could not tell what effect it had on the enemy machine.

'As I pulled up into a steep right-hand curving turn I saw a burning aeroplane in a dive off to my left. I could not follow its progress any longer as I observed four more I-153s coming towards me. One of these fighters was flying a bit higher than the others, and as I gained altitude it made a gentle turn to the right. This allowed me to get into a firing position from side-on, and this improved as I continued to get in behind and slightly beneath the higher I-153. I saw my bursts hit the enemy aircraft, which began to trail smoke before it fell away in a dive, seemingly out of control. When this encounter took place we were between the layers of clouds. I could not follow the aircraft down to the deck, however. My own aeroplane, FR-130, suffered no damage.'

On 15 April the D.XXIs of 2/LLv 30 shot up seven trucks carrying fuel on the ice road between Seiskari and Harjavalta, setting them alight. They also sent down one of two 'Chaikas' that appeared on the scene, Capt Veikko Karu claiming the fighter;

'At 0820 hrs, whilst I was flying a CAP mission with six aeroplanes over lake Lempaalanjärvi at an altitude of 1500 metres [4900 ft], I observed an aircraft slightly below me south over Lumisuo. Its pilot saw me, too, and he began to gain altitude in an attempt to escape until he realised that he could not shake me off. At this point he turned towards me. Moments later another I-153 flashed beneath me, heading south. I continued my attack against the first fighter, however.

'We were flying over Perämäki at the time, and the Russian began shooting slightly earlier as we raced head-on towards each other. I held my fire until I had the I-153 squarely in my gunsight, at which point I shot off a long burst that hit the fighter's engine. My opponent stopped firing as soon as the first bullets hit his aircraft. Moments later the I-153 flipped onto its port wing and light smoke began trailing from the engine. I had time to shoot into the cockpit when the aircraft rolled onto its side in front of me. When the Russian fighter flashed past me I saw that it was smoking pretty well.

'The pilot then made a left curving turn, which I could not follow due to the excessive speed I had gained when diving at the I-153. Indeed, I would have blacked out had I tried to turn after him. When I next saw the enemy fighter it was diving at about a 45-degree angle south at an altitude of about 300 metres [1000 ft]. I decided to go after it, but then I saw four enemy aircraft above me to the south – I did not observe the type. I began to gain altitude on them instead, at which point they broke off and headed home. I too decided to return to our side of the frontline. There were no hits on my aeroplane, as the short burst that the enemy had fired went over me. My aeroplane was FR-129.'

LLv 30 units saw little action for the rest of April, and in May its squadron abbreviation changed from LLv to LeLv. The frontline on the Karelian Isthmus was reconnoitred two or three times a week, and other duties were performed as required. The squadron's area of operations was specified as the Viipuri-Lavansaari-Seivästö sector. The summer months passed by quietly, with only routine missions being flown, and on 9 October LeLv 30 completed its 4000th sortie. The most significant event of this period occurred on 6 November when 2/LeLv 30 leader Capt Veikko Karu was awarded the Mannerheim Cross (Finland's highest

Below right
Lentue Kää r's deputy leader, 1Lt Martti Kalima, stands proudly alongside the tally on the rudder of his aircraft, FR-148, at Tiiksjärvi in March 1942. The scoreboard records all of the claims made by pilots flying this aeroplane, three of which were credited to Kalima. He scored four victories flying D.XXIs and 6.5 in MS.406s (*R Rosenberg*)

Below left
Kalima's personal emblem, Pinocchio, was portrayed on both sides of the fin. A pre-war step dance champion in Finland, Kalima's military merit lay in him being the *Ilmavoimat's* top-scoring fighter pilot in eastern Karelia (*R Rosenberg*)

military decoration). Credited with seven aerial victories, he had also shared in the sinking of 13 surface vessels.

A fortnight later the squadron received new equipment in the form of captured I-153 fighters bought from Germany. The D.XXIs kept flying with LeLv 30 until the end of March 1943, however, after which they performed reconnaissance missions only. The unit's final tally with the D.XXI was 33 Soviet aircraft shot down.

Flown by the leader of 1/LLv 10, Capt Pekka Käär, FR-144 was photographed at Tiiksjärvi on 4 October 1941. Instead of a tactical number, Käär chose the letter 'A'. This flight had previously been 3/LLv 30, which it again formally became on 1 November 1941, although with the name *Lentue* Käär and subordinated to LLv 14 (*SA-kuva*)

EASTERN KARELIAN EPISODE

LLv 10 was formed on 12 August 1941 as the northernmost flying unit of the *Ilmavoimat*. Based at Tiiksjärvi, right next to the German sector of the frontline, the squadron commenced operations on 1 September. It was initially tasked with performing reconnaissance missions for the 14th Division over Rukajärvi. LLv 10 consisted of a fighter and a reconnaissance flight, the former being equipped with Hurricanes from 1/LLv 30 until they were replaced by six D.XXIs from 3/LLv 30 on 21 September. This flight was then re-designated 1/LLv 10.

Two days later 1/LLv 10 was twice engaged in combat with 'Chaikas' over Rukajärvi. In the first clash 1Lt Aaro Virkkunen's *swarm* sent one of eight Soviet aircraft down, and in the second Capt Erkki Ilveskorpi's five D.XXIs fought with a dozen I-153s, setting one alight. On 27 September 1Lt Martti Kalima's 1/LLv 10 was scrambled to intercept four I-153s over Ontajoki, the squadron's combat report on the action stating;

FR-146 of *Lentue* Käär has its armament harmonised at Tiiksjärvi in March 1942. This fighter was assigned to Cpl Hemmo Leino, who used it to claim a LaGG-3 on 9 January 1942 and a shared R-5 ten days later. Leino was eventually credited with 11 kills in total (*T Vuorinen*)

'On an alert mission between 0925-1025 hrs we flew towards the front with eight aircraft. The lower patrol, consisting of 1Lt Kalima (FR-150), 2Lts Salomaa (FR-154) and Virtanen (FR-155) and Sgts Nuorala (FR-148) and Kilpinen (FR-141), flew at an altitude of about 100 metres [330 ft]. The upper patrol, comprising 1Lt Lehtonen (FR-156) and 2Lts Ukkonen (FR-153) and Leino (FR-138), were some 200 metres [660 ft] higher.

'The top patrol leader, 1Lt Lehtonen, observed five Russian fighters of I-153 type to the east over the frontline. We were about five kilometres [three miles] from them. Lehtonen tried to inform the lower patrol of his observations, but 2Lt Salomaa, flying on the left wing of the lower patrol, had already seen the enemy and informed his formation leader, 1Lt Kalima. We turned towards them and tried to gain more altitude, as the Russians were already at a height of 500 metres [1600 ft]. Only four enemy aircraft remained – one had broken off earlier, leaving the others heading east in a shallow climb.

'Upon seeing us they turned in our direction and dived in a line towards us with an altitude advantage of 150 metres [500 ft]. Our own aircraft were in an inclined echelon caused by our banking turn and the fact that the top patrol had just tried to inform the lower aircraft about the Russian formation. We pulled into them and started firing. After the initial head-on pass, we banked around tightly and went after them in a "blind combat", which saw the more manoeuvrable Russian pilots, in spite of their inferior numbers, always getting onto the tail of a D.XXI. We were saved by our good tactical training, however, for every time a Russian aeroplane got onto the tail of one of our aircraft, another Fokker pilot would open fire at it.

'Nevertheless, at the very outset of the engagement a bullet came through the windscreen of 1Lt Lehtonen's aircraft and exploded upon entering the cockpit. He was forced to break off, bullet splinters having

D.XII FR-148 of *Lentue* Käär, seconded to LLv 14, is seen at Tiiksjärvi on 4 November 1941. It was assigned to the deputy leader, 1Lt Martti Kalima. The fighter had only been fitted with skis several hours prior to this photograph being taken, hence their clean appearance. Most of Lentue Käär's aircraft were ski-equipped that same day (*SA-kuva*)

damaged his eyes so badly that his sight was blurred. Moments later 2Lt Ukkonen shot at an I-153 that flew towards him for so long that he had time to make a small evasive manoeuvre – this was just as well, for his Russian opponent flew straight on. 2Lt Ukkonen's undercarriage took off the port upper wing of the I-153, which crashed. Ukkonen had great difficulty regaining control of his aircraft and he too was forced to break off the fight. His machine then caught fire and he had to bail out 20 km [12 miles] from the frontline in friendly territory.

'The remaining six D.XXI pilots continued to fight for their lives. An I-153 worked its way onto the tail of Sgt Kilpinen's Fokker, firing at him. Seeing his squadronmate in trouble, 1Lt Kalima got in behind the Russian and gave him a burst. The enemy pilot ceased firing and pulled up into a shallow climbing turn, whereupon Kalima fired another burst while turning with the I-153 and it crashed in flames in a pond. Free of his opponent, Sgt Kilpinen manoeuvred in behind another banking I-153 and fired at it until the aircraft caught fire and crashed. 2Lt Salomaa got behind the last remaining I-153 and opened fire, but his foe escaped in a high-speed dive, despite his fighter emitting smoke.'

On 1 November LLv 10 became part of reconnaissance squadron LLv 14, which had been sent to Tiiksjärvi with two flights of Mercury-powered D.XXIs.

On Christmas Eve three Soviet SB bombers, escorted by six Hurricanes, made a low-level attack on Tiiksjärvi. A patrol of LLv 14 aircraft happened to be airborne at the time, and 1Lt Toivo Vuorinen's combat report stated;

'The three of us attacked from out of the sun against the six-aeroplane Hurricane patrol, only one of which fired back. I shot at one Hurricane from 50 metres [165 ft] while it was making a climbing turn. The aircraft then fell away trailing thick smoke. Two more Soviet fighters fired at me from my right side and directly ahead, but they missed. I then dived for the ground and chased after the Hurricanes that were fleeing eastwards. They were faster than me, however, and the distance between us kept increasing all the time, despite one of the aircraft emitting smoke. I continued the chase, in FR-105, until I broke off for home east of Rukajärvi.'

On 19 January 1942 1Lt Veijo Taina and his wingman from LLv 14 flew a reconnaissance mission from Lentue Käär to Ontajärvi. An R-5 spotted on the ice was strafed and another that managed to get airborne was quickly shot down. Taina's combat report stated;

'I was on patrol between 0810-0910 hrs, at an altitude of 200 metres [650 ft], with Cpl Leino in FR-146. He was 300 metres [980 ft] higher and slightly behind me on the right. Spotting the Soviet biplanes, I pushed the nose of my fighter down a little and opened fire from 100 metres [325 ft]. The aeroplane banked immediately to the left and its nose went down. Cpl Leino also made a similar attack, after which the engine of the enemy aeroplane cut and the propeller blades stopped. Before it hit the ice, we had time to repeat our attacks. The observer fired back, and when the aircraft hit the ice he and the pilot jumped out and ran for cover. I was flying FR-156.'

By March 1942 the VVS and Naval Air Forces units in-theatre had received considerable reinforcements via the railway line that ran directly from the port of Murmansk. Indeed, on 10 March a formation of Hurricanes bounced a pair of D.XXIs from 1/LLv 14 near lake Tungutjärvi

2Lt Mikko Salomaa climbs into the cockpit of D.XXI FR-156 of 1/LLv 10 at Tiiksjärvi on 25 September 1941. Although the rudder bears a victory mark, Salomaa scored only one kill in this aircraft – an R-5 biplane on 22 July 1942 (*SA-kuva*)

and shot them both down. Following this episode reconnaissance missions over the railway were avoided.

On 14 April a Soviet U-2 biplane was forced down by bad weather on the ice of Tiiksjärvi well after midnight. Two D.XXIs from LLv 14 were sent to find the aircraft, which they duly discovered had landed in the middle of a frozen lake. It was quickly destroyed. In the weak dawn light the fighter pilots had failed to observe a five-man Finnish Army patrol that had reached the aeroplane five minutes before they strafed it!

Fifteen days later 1Lt Martti Kalima and his wingman, Sgt Aaro Nuorala, were reconnoitring Tunkua when a nine-aircraft fighter detachment surprised the Finns. In the fierce aerial battle that ensued Nuorala shot one of the Hurricanes down. Both Fokker pilots succeeded in breaking off the engagement, but not before their D.XXIs had been riddled by enemy fire. The aircraft returned with the tyres punctured by bullets, and landed without further damage – groundcrews counted more than 50 bullet holes in each fighter. The Hurricane pilots of 152nd IAP erroneously reported having shot down two Fokkers in the Rukajärvi area.

Just after midnight on 22 July three D.XXIs from Osasto Käär-based LeLv 14 were sent aloft to ambush Soviet R-5 supply aircraft. They encountered two of them and one was shot down, the other biplane managing to flee under the cover of the twilight sky. In his combat report 2Lt Mikko Salomaa wrote;

'Between 0040-0140 hrs, we searched over Lake Voijärvi at an altitude of 50 metres [160 ft]. I saw an enemy aeroplane when we flew over Pekonvaara Hill, the biplane heading west at a tree-top level of 5-10 metres [16-30 ft]. I banked around onto its tail and fired a burst, during which the observer was killed and the aeroplane caught fire. I then pulled up and circled above it. When I saw the burning aeroplane trying to dodge the firing passes made by my comrades, I targeted it with another burst. The aircraft then flipped over and crashed into the forest. I was flying FR-156.'

From August LeLv 14 began to receive MS.406 fighters that had been acquired from stocks seized by the Germans in occupied France. These machines had then been thoroughly refurbished by the Finnish State Aircraft Factory. The D.XXIs were relegated to the reconnaissance role,

81

and it was whilst performing this mission on 23 December that a pair of Fokker fighters from 2/LeLv 14 claimed the type's final aerial victory with the unit. 1Lt Veli Hakola recalled;

'Aloft between 1250-1350 hrs, at an altitude of 100 metres [330 ft], we spotted an R-5 biplane over the shore of Nuokkijärvi, about eight kilometres [five miles] east of Pääkköniemi. Flying a curving approach, I quickly got in behind and above the aeroplane. After seeing its red stars I fired a burst at it. The aircraft soon began to trail white smoke [probably fuel from the punctured upper tank] as it tried to head for Nuokkijärvi, losing altitude as it went.

'Flying at low level around a higher spit of land, 2Lt Lilja fired at the biplane as it attempted to turn in for landing. I fired another burst into the aircraft before the pilot managed to touch down, however, causing the biplane to erupt in flames. When its skis touched the snow it flipped over and continued to burn fiercely. Moments later I observed an airman pull his wounded comrade into the forest for cover. I was flying FR-135.'

This proved to be the last aerial victory credited anywhere to the venerable D.XXI. Fokker pilots did still shoot at aeroplanes, however, but in strafing passes. This was indeed what happened on 12 January 1943 when three D.XXIs from 3/LeLv 14, led by 1Lt Mikko Nysten, reconnoitred the field outpost line north of Uhtua and, from there, south to the main road;

'On patrol from 1000-1120 hrs, mainly at an altitude of 500 metres [1640 ft]. South of Röhöjärvi, we could not spot any vehicle tracks in the

Photographs providing a clear view of uppersurface camouflage are scarce, but this unique shot reveals the scheme worn by FR-140. Seen flying over Lake Onega's northern area in the summer of 1942, the aeroplane belonged to *Lentue* Käär of LLv 14 (*R Rosenberg*)

FR-98 of 1/LLv 12 at Nurmoila in early 1942. The 1st Flight had its ram emblem painted on the forward fuselage, while the tail number is a relic from the machine's time with 1/LLv 32 (*Finnish Air Force Museum*)

snow. The road coming from the southeast to Kiiskjoki village had been used, however. We also spotted a sleigh track from the east to Haapajärvi, continuing via the southern end of the village to the west. There was nothing special to report between Haapajärvi and Mikkola. On the road at Mikkola airfield we saw three trucks heading westward, which we strafed. At Mikkola airfield eight R-5s with bombs under their wings were parked in shelters. Two in shelters on the northern edge of the airfield faced west and six on the narrow forest strip along the southern edge of the airfield faced north. We attacked, and after several strafing runs three aeroplanes on the south side had caught fire and were burning fiercely. Others were strafed too, but with no visual effect. The attack was called off once we had used up all of our ammunition.'

Nysten informed his superiors at Tiiksjärvi of his success over the radio and 1/LeLv 14 leader Capt Martti Tainio was scrambled from Mikkola airfield at 1200 hrs with five MS.406s so as to finish off the remaining R-5s. Once over the Soviet base Tainio and his men observed one R-5 on fire, and then strafed a second one that was parked next to it. After rearming and refuelling, Nysten's patrol took off again from Kiantajärvi and headed back to Mikkola;

'On the southern edge of the airfield we strafed two aircraft until they were alight, and repeated this treatment on a third machine parked on the northern edge. Another biplane sat nearby was also strafed, and it too caught fire. However, enemy personnel managed to extinguish the fire shortly after our attack. One aircraft on the southern edge remained intact. Our aircraft suffered six rifle-calibre hits. The enemy's anti-aircraft defences seemed to consist of just three machine guns.'

RECONNAISSANCE

LLv 12 received its D.XXIs from LLv 32 during the third week of July 1941. The squadron was then instructed to reconnoitre for the 100,000-man strong Karelian Army, which was tasked with retaking the territory

lost to the Soviet Union in the peace treaty that brought an end to the
Winter War. While LLv 12 flew missions over the right sector of the front,
the Gladiators of LLv 16 covered the left sector.

The Karelian Army reached the River Tuulos on 23 July and temporarily
halted its advance. On 4 September the drive to the River Svir, linking
Lakes Onega and Ladoga, began. Two days later eight aircraft of LLv 12
reconnoitred the water routes and roads heading to Lotinanpelto and
carried out a low-level strafing attack on retreating Soviet troops and
motorised columns on the Mäkriä-Lotinanpelto road, destroying around
20 trucks. The aeroplanes (and pilots) involved were FR-91 (Capt
Maunula), FR-92 (Capt Metsola), FR-103 (1Lt Ritavuori), FR-114 (1Lt
Mustonen), FR-98 (2Lt Marttila), FR-83 (2Lt Mäenpää), FR-117 (SSgt
Juhola) and FR-95 (Sgt Koskivirta). Some 5375 rounds of 7.7 mm
ammunition were expended, and when six I-153s appeared on the scene
1Lt Ilpo Ritavuori shot one of them down;

'I had just attacked a column of cars next to the road at Troitsankontu
when, after climbing to an altitude of about 700 metres [2300 ft], I observed
an I-153 about 1000 metres [3280 ft] away darting behind a small cumulus
cloud ahead of me off to my left side. He was about 50 metres [160 ft]
higher than I was, and turning in towards me. I pulled my nose in the
direction of the cloud, banking left at the same time. I then saw the I-153
again, coming towards me from behind the left side of the cloud. It banked
to the left and I banked too, the fighter coming into view through my
gunsight. I opened fire and my bullets hit the side if the aircraft, causing it
to burst into flames. The I-153 dived away trailing smoke.

'As I turned to chase after it, I spotted another "Chaika" coming after me some 500 metres [1640 ft] away. I pushed over into a dive and made an aileron turn. The I-153 continued to chase me at ground level, but it failed to get any closer than 1000 metres [3280 ft]. I then flew into a rainstorm and lost the I-153. My aeroplane was FR-103.'

By 23 October the whole of the River Svir was in Finnish possession, and a stalemate began. The enemy was occasionally seen on regular reconnaissance missions, as an encounter on 10 November shows. In his combat report 2Lt Lauri Hovilainen of 2/LLv 12 wrote;

'I was the lead aeroplane of a pair on a reconnaissance mission from Larishna to Vodlitsa, flying along the road that connected the two villages at an altitude of 1000 metres [3280 ft]. Over the village I observed a two-seat biplane aircraft of the R-5 type turning south just below us. I put my aeroplane into a vertical dive and raced after it, firing a short burst at the banking aircraft. When I levelled out I saw the observer hanging over the side of the fuselage in the direction the aircraft was turning. I made a climbing turn and saw my wingman attack the enemy aeroplane, which was heading to the east above the treetops.

'When my wingman pulled up I saw that the enemy aeroplane was still aloft, so I again dived onto its tail just as the machine started to turn a little to the left. I fired a short burst from a distance of 50-80 metres [165-260 ft], after which black smoke came pouring out from the aircraft's engine. Its nose then nose dipped suddenly towards the ground and the biplane crashed into the forest. There had been no return fire from the aircraft at any point in the engagement.

'A bright yellow band about 70 cm [28 in] in width was painted around the fuselage just aft of the observer's position, and there were red stars on the wingtips. The battle had begun at 1250 hrs. My aeroplane was FR-95.'

FR-92 of 2/LeLv 12 at Nurmoila on 2 August 1942. The 2nd Flight had a donkey emblem. Note also that the tail markings of former owner LLv 32 have been covered with fresh paint (*Finnish Air Force*)

Again, on 18 December, a pair of D.XXIs from 1/LLv 12 on a reconnaissance mission intercepted an R-5 at 0945 hrs near Osta, as 1Lt Oiva Tylli, flying FR-98, reported;

'I was flying at a height of 500 metres [1640 ft], heading northwest, with my wingman about 100 metres [330 ft] to my right and behind me, when I saw an R-5 on my right side just 100 metres away at ground level, heading southeast. I signalled my wingman (Sgt Matilainen) and half-rolled after the R-5. I shot a long burst at the aircraft, but as my gun armed with tracer was inoperable, my aim was not accurate enough. The enemy aircraft was in a shallow banking turn throughout my attack.

'I pulled up alongside the biplane, and at the same time saw my wingman make a pass at it. When he too failed to bring the R-5 down, I dived after it again and opened fire from about 50 metres [165 ft]. The aeroplane then banked over and fell into the forest. I did not see the gunner fire a single round at us.'

On 8 January 1942 Finnish troops took more ground from the enemy in Gora village, on the River Svir. Later that day, when the weather improved, 1/LLv 12 flew a reconnaissance mission to ascertain whether the Red Army was going to attempt to seize back the ground it had lost. As 2Lt Ossi Marttila and his wingman approached Gora they were intercepted by four MiG-3 fighters from 415th IAP. The D.XXI pilots pulled over into a dive and saw three Russian aircraft at ground level. One was shot at and began to smoke, after which the Finnish pilots hastily returned to base. The damaged MiG-3 subsequently crash-landed.

On 19 February a pair of D.XXIs from LLv 12 engaged two R-5s and sent both of them down, Maj Auvo Maunula's combat report stating;

'I was flying the lead aeroplane in a mid-morning patrol, and as we approached Aleksevskaya I saw two R-5s flying towards us in an easterly direction near the Ojattijoki River. They were above us at an altitude of 150 metres [490 ft]. I did not immediately start an attack because I did not want my wingman, Sgt Jankko, and I subjected to enemy anti-aircraft artillery. Sgt Jankko had also seen the aircraft, and he informed me of this by waving in my direction.

'I continued flying at low-level and then banked over the Ojattijoki River so as to get the sun at our backs. As we turned about a kilometre in front of the R-5s their pilots obviously saw us, as they descended towards the riverbed. The latter was in a steep ravine, thus ruling out an attack from the flank. We therefore had to attack from immediately behind. I initially fired a short burst at the rearmost aeroplane from 100 metres [330 ft] and then followed up with continuous fire from 50 metres (165 ft). This had no effect on the R-5, as it avoided my fire by banking steeply to starboard. I then banked to port and made another attack.

'Since I had failed to achieve any success by firing from behind, I shot a short burst from 200 metres [660 ft] so as to persuade the pilot to bank. This he did, to port, whereupon I was able to shoot the aircraft in the port side at short range. The aircraft was then at an altitude of just five metres [15 ft], and it went over onto its port wing towards the forest on the river bank. I did not see the R-5 crash because I had to suddenly pull up to port so as to avoid the aeroplane, and the trees it flew into.

'After completing a tight banking turn and preparing myself for the next attack, I spotted the remaining aircraft and went after it from directly behind. I intended to get as close to the R-5 as possible so that the aeroplane could not straighten out before Sgt Jankko shot at it from the side. I decreased engine revs as much as I could and fired until I had to pull up steeply to port to avoid colliding with the biplane, which, by then, was in a steep banking turn to starboard. It was at this point that Sgt Jankko, flying about 100 metres behind me, managed to shoot straight into the flank of the R-5. After pulling up I could not see the aircraft any more – it had crash-landed in a field at Kuzdra following Sgt Jankko's attack. I was flying aeroplane FR-98.'

On 24 April two more D.XXIs from 2/LLv 12 found a pair of R-5s from 5th OAP (*Osobaya Aviatsionnaya Polk* – Special Aviation Regiment) on a reconnaissance mission. Both R-5s were shot down, one being claimed by 1Lt Oiva Tylli;

'I was leading a morning patrol, with Sgt Koskivirta as my wingman, southeast along the Lotinanpelto-Alehovchina road at an altitude of about 1000 metres [3300 ft] when I observed two R-5s flying southeast at a height of 100 metres [330 ft] north of Alehovchina. I half-rolled into a dive towards one of them and fired a short burst obliquely from the side and behind at a distance of 50 metres [165 ft]. The rear gunner managed to fire a few rounds back at me, but after my first shots hit the R-5 he stopped. At the same time the aeroplane entered a shallow banking turn to port, descending until it made a forced landing in a field and flipped over onto its back. I then strafed the biplane and it burst into flames. I saw one crewman run for cover in a nearby forest.

'From this engagement I learnt that the R-5 must be shot at either from the side or obliquely from behind because armour plating protects both the

For D.XXI top-scorer Capt Jorma Sarvanto, his wartime connection with the Fokker fighter continued into the last weeks of the Continuation War, when he was made Chief Instructor of 2/T-LeLv 35, an advanced training squadron. His aeroplane was FR-156, seen at Kauhava in August 1944 (*Finnish Air Museum*)

pilot and the engine. The pilot did not make any obvious manoeuvres prior to me attacking him, and after I had hit his aircraft he performed a shallow turn in an attempt to evade. My aeroplane, FR-92, suffered no damage.'

On 20 July a three-aeroplane patrol from 2/LeLv 12 was engaged by an identical number of LaGG-3 fighters over Lotinanpelto. In the ensuing action both sides lost an aircraft, as Sgt Oiva Hietala recalled;

'We were on a morning reconnaissance mission, with 2Lt Miettinen flying the lead aeroplane, Sgt Kalervo as his wingman and me as top cover. We were on the south side of Lotinanpelto when I observed three enemy fighters approaching us from the east at an altitude of about 2200 m (7210 ft) altitude. I was then at 2400 metres [7,875 ft] and the lead aeroplane was at 2000 metres [6,560 ft]. I signalled the lead aeroplane and made a climbing turn, firing at the enemy fighters from the rear and above from a range of 50 metres [55 yd]. I saw my stream of tracers hit the aircraft behind the engine and cockpit. The enemy fighter disappeared beneath me and I did not see it again. A column of smoke rose in the direction of Savijärvi – I assumed that the enemy aircraft had crashed there.

'I began a turning fight with the two remaining aircraft, getting into a firing position several times, but only at a distance. I saw that Sgt Kalervo managed to shoot at one from very close range in a head-on pass, after which the Russian fighter broke away and left the scene. 2Lt Miettinen did not return to the base. I was flying FR-92.'

On 24 August 1942 Maj Auvo Maunula, who had commanded LLv 12 for a year, was made CO of MS.406-equipped LeLv 28. Two weeks later he was awarded the Mannerheim Cross for his achievements both as a reconnaissance pilot and leader. He eventually finished the war with three aerial victories to his credit.

Surviving D.XXIs continued to perform the armed reconnaissance mission until the armistice on 4 September 1944. Their service to the *Ilmavoimat* was not yet over, however, as the Air Fighting School continued to use ten D.XXIs until 13 September 1948, when they were put into storage and eventually scrapped four years later.

APPENDICES

Finnish Fokker D.XXI Aces

Name	Rank	Unit	Fokker score	Total score	Remarks
J K Sarvanto	Lt	4/LLv 24	13	17	
P E Sovelius	1Lt	4/LLv 24	7.75	14.75	
V Pyötsiä	WO	3/LLv 24	7.5	21.5	
T M Huhanantti	1Lt	3/LLv 24	7	7	KIA 29/2/40
V J Karu*	Capt	2/LLv 30	6.75	10.75	MHR
J Karhunen	1Lt	2/LLv 24	6.5	31.5	(MHR)
K T Virta	MSgt	2/LLv 24	6	6	(KIFA 28/1/41)
P T Tilli*	SSgt	3/LLv 24	5	5	KIA 20/1/40
U A Nieminen*	1Lt	5/LLv 24	5	11	
L V Nissinen	SSgt	5/LLv 24	5	32.5	(MHR, KIA 17/6/44)
R O P Puhakka*	2Lt	1/LLv 24	5	46	(MHR)
T O Vuorimaa	2Lt	1/LLv 24	5	5	

Finnish Aces with Fokker D.XXI victories

Name	Rank	Unit	Fokker score	Total score	Remarks
Y O Turkka	WO	1/LLv 24	4.75	17.5	
M T J Kalima	1Lt	3/LLv 30	4	10.5	
P J Kokko	2Lt	2/LLv 24	4	13.5	(KIFA 19/2/44)
G E Magnusson	Maj	E/LLv 24	4	5.5	(MHR)
E A Kinnunen	Sgt	1/LLv 24	3.5	22.5	(KIA 21/4/43)
A E Nuorala	Sgt	2/LLv 30	3	14.5	
T A Mattila	2Lt	2/LLv 30	2.75	5.75	
V A Evinen	1Lt	1/LLv 32	2.5	6	(KIA 25/6/44)
E A Luukkanen	Capt	3/LLv 24	2.5	54	(MHR)
L E Aaltonen*	Sgt	5/LLv 24	2	13.5	
E I Juutilainen	Sgt	3/LLv 24	2	94	(MHR twice)
O K Paronen*	Sgt	5/LLv 24	2	10.5	
H S Ikonen	MSgt	4/LLv 24	1.75	6.5	
M A Alho	Sgt	3/LLv 24	1.5	13.5	(KIFA 5/6/43)
H K Leino	Sgt	3/LLv 30	1.5	11	
V J Rimminen	MSgt	2/LLv 24	1.5	6	
O E K Tuominen*	SSgt	2/LLv 24	1.5	47	(MHR)
E O Ehrnrooth**	Capt	KoeL	1	5	(KIFA 27/2/43)
M M Fräntilä	SSgt	3/LLv 24	1	5	
M I Kirjonen	Cpl	2/LLv 32	1	9.75	
I V Törrönen	2Lt	4/LLv 24	1	11	(KIA 2/5/43)
P E Salminen	SSgt	1/LLv 32	0.5	6	
A H T Maunula	Maj	E/LLv 12	1	3	(MHR, KIFA 17/5/44)

Key

* – denotes on assignment from LLv 26

** – test pilot

MHR – Mannerheim Cross

KIA – Killed in action

KIFA – Killed in flying accident

The rank given in these tables is the one held at the time of the pilot's last claim with the D.XXI. The unit stated is the one in which the majority of their Fokker victories were scored. Remarks mentioned in parenthesis refer to another unit or a later period. These victory totals are in some instances slightly different from those published in earlier *Osprey Aircraft of the Aces* and *Aviation Elite Units* books. Since their publication in 1998 and 2001, respectively, new information has emerged from the Russian archives, and a handful of claims recorded as damaged have been upgraded to confirmed victories

Dutch D.XXI aerial victories

Date/Area	Pilot/Unit/Aircraft	Victim	Status	Remarks
19 November 1939 Schiermonnikoog Island	Lt H van Overvest 'White Mice' 1st JaVA ?	He 111H 7A+CH 1.(F)/121	Confirmed	Crash-landed on Borkum Island
10 May 1940 NE of The Hague	Lt A van der Vaart Field Army 1st JaVA 212	Do 17Z Aufkl.St. 7 Fl.Div 4Q+JH	Confirmed	Crashed near Wilnis
10 May 1940 The Hague	Lt F Droste Field Army 1st JaVA 228	Ju 88A 5./KG 30 4D+BN	Confirmed	
10 May 1940 The Hague	Sgt G Kiel Field Army 1st JaVA 216	Ju 52/3m IV./KGzbV 1	Probable	
10 May 1940 The Hague	Sgt P Aarts Field Army 1st JaVA 217	Bf 110C II./ZG 1	Damaged	
10 May 1940 The Hague	Sgt J Eden Field Army 1st JaVA 247	Bf 110C II./ZG 1	Damaged	
10 May 1940 The Hague	Sgt J Linzel Field Army 1st JaVA 246	Bf 110C II./ZG 1	Damaged	
10 May 1940 Leiden	Sgt W Hateboer 'White Mice' 1st JaVA 244	Ju 52/3m	Probable	Crash-landed on beach
10 May 1940 Den Helder	Lt H Doppenberg 'White Mice' 1st JaVA 221	Bf 109E 5./JG 186 Uffz W Rudolf	Confirmed	Crashed southeast of Den Helder
10 May 1940 Den Helder	Lt H van Overvest 'White Mice' 1st JaVA 219	Bf 109E 5./JG 186 Hptm D Robitzsch	Confirmed	Crash-landed De Kooy
10 May 1940 Den Helder	Lt F Focquin de Grave 'White Mice' 1st JaVA 218	Bf 109E 5./JG 186	Shared	Crash-landed on Borkum Island
10 May 1940 Den Helder	Lt B van der Stok 'White Mice' 1st JaVA 234	as above	Shared	as above
10 May 1940 Gouda	Sgt B de Geus 2nd JaVA 236	Ju 52/3m 3./KGrzbV 9 9P+DL	Shared	Crashed near Stolwijk

10 May 1940 Gouda	Lt H Plesman 2nd JaVA 235	as above	Shared	as above
10 May 1940 Schiphol	Lt N Sluijter 2nd JaVA 225	Ju 88A 9./KG 4 5J+GT	Confirmed	Crashed near Hoofddorp
11 May 1940 NE of Rotterdam	Lt F Focquin de Grave Combined JaVA 213	Bf 110C 3./ZG 1	Confirmed	Crashed near Gorinchem

Totals

H van Overvest – 2

F Focquin de Grave – 1.5

H Doppenberg, F Droste, N Sluijter and A van der Vaart – 1

W Hateboer and G Kiel – 1 probable

B de Geus, H Plesman and B van der Stok – 0.5

P Aarts, J Eden and J Linzel – 1 damaged

COLOUR PLATES

1

D.XXI No 232 (c/n 5505) of Lt F L M Focquin de Grave, 1st JaVA, Eelde, 13 September 1939

The D.XXI's baptism of fire occurred on 13 September 1939 when both Holland and Finland were still at peace. Following an incident in which a Dutch T.VIIIW seaplane was shot down off Schiermonnikoog Island, an alighted Do 18 flying boat (M2+LK) was strafed by 1st JaVA flight leader Frans Focquin de Grave. The crew were interned. The Dutch national insignia was changed from a roundel to an orange triangle, with orange rudders after these events. Rudders had originally been red, white and blue, but they were painted in camouflage colours in accordance with a decree issued on 5 December 1938. Assigned to the 2nd JaVA in May 1940, No 232 was unserviceable when Germany invaded Holland and was duly captured by the Wehrmacht at Schiphol Airport.

2

D.XXI No 212 (c/n 5485) of Lt A M van der Vaart, Field Army 1st JaVA, Ypenburg, 10 May 1940

The first D.XXI delivered to the Dutch Army's *Luchtvaartafdeling* (Aviation Branch), this aircraft made its maiden flight on 26 May 1938. In January 1940 it was assigned to the Field Army 1st JaVA, and during the morning of 10 May the aircraft was the mount of Lt A M van der Vaart, who chased and shot down Do 17Z reconnaissance aircraft 4Q+JH. Van der Vaart subsequently landed at Schiphol, and his was the only D.XXI of the Field Army 1st JaVA to survive the initial German onslaught. Added to the combined squadron at Buiksloot, the aircraft flew five more sorties, and was one of the nine D.XXIs destroyed by the Dutch themselves at Schiphol on 14 May.

3

D.XXI No 228 (c/n 5501) of Lt F G B Droste, Field Army 1st JaVA, Ypenburg, 10 May 1940

Lt Droste was among the first pilots assigned to the Field Army 1st JaVA, a unit officially raised at Soesterberg on 6 November 1939. It moved to Eindhoven on 16 March 1940 and then to Ypenburg, near The Hague, on 10 April. Leading a two-aircraft flight on 10 May, Droste shot down a Ju 88 of 5./KG 30. With his wingman, Sgt Aarts, he then landed at Ockenburg airfield, which was invaded by airborne troops shortly thereafter, rendering the two D.XXIs unusable. Droste escaped to Schiphol, and ended his May war flying a Twin Wasp Junior-powered Fokker G.I fighter on 14 May.

4

D.XXI No 247 (c/n 5520) of Sgt J Eden, Field Army 1st JaVA, Ypenburg, 10 May 1940

The final D.XXI built in the Netherlands, No 247 was delivered to the Field Army 1st JaVA. On 10 May 1940 it was assigned to Sgt Jaap Eden, who damaged a Bf 110 of II./ZG I whilst flying it. Landing back at Ypenburg amid a ground battle, Eden was quickly captured by German paratroopers and the aircraft destroyed. The pilot was liberated by Dutch troops a few hours later. Jaap Eden was the son of a famous father, Jaap Eden Snr, a speed-skating and cycling world champion of the 1890s.

5

D.XXI No 223 (c/n 5496) of *Wachtmeester* J van Zuijlen, 'White Mice' 1st JaVA, De Kooy, 10 May 1940

First flown on 7 October 1938, No 223 was transferred from the 2nd JaVA to the 'White Mice' 1st JaVA in 1940, receiving the appropriate marking on the port side of its nose. The 'Pointed shoes!' yell seen below the cockpit was displayed on a number of the unit's aircraft. This airframe was not yet radio equipped on 10 May – a fact that may have contributed to the death of *Wachtmeester* (cavalry sergeant) Jaap 'Jacky' van Zuijlen, as he did not follow his leader when his flight was called back to De Kooy. Van Zuijlen was presumably killed by a He 111 gunner before No 223 crashed in the coastal dunes at Wassenaarseslag, north of The Hague.

6

D.XXI No 235 (c/n 5508) of Lt J C Hans Plesman, 2nd JaVA, Schiphol, 10 May 1940

The eldest son of KLM president Albert Plesman, Hans Plesman was a flight leader of the 2nd JaVA at Schiphol and saw a lot of action during the May war. He shared in the destruction of Ju 52/3m 9P+DL with Sgt De Geus on 10 May, and logged more operational flying hours than any other Dutch D.XXI pilot, completing nine sorties in total. Seven of these were flown in No 235, which was also used by Bob van der Stok on one occasion. The aircraft was destroyed by the Dutch on 14 May. Hans Plesman's younger brother, Jan, flew the D.XXI as a student fighter pilot and completed one operational mission in a D.XVII on 12 May 1940. Jan was killed in action in a Spitfire of No 322 (Dutch) Sqn over France in 1944. Hans became a KLM captain and lost his life in the crash of a Lockheed L-749 Constellation near Bari in 1949.

7

D.XXI No 213 (c/n 5486) of Lt F L M Focquin de Grave, Combined JaVA, Buiksloot, 11 May 1940

Assigned to the 2nd JaVA, No 213 was the mount of Sgt Gé Burger during the early morning patrol of 10 May, and it was then flown on two missions from Ruigenhoek by Lt Hans Plesman, who used the fighter to share in the destruction of a Ju 52/3m. It was ferried to Buiksloot airfield, in North Amsterdam, by Burger, and the next day the fighter flew two escort missions to Rotterdam as the flight leader's aircraft, with Lt Bik at the controls in the morning and Lt Focquin de Grave in the early afternoon. Twelve Bf 110s were encountered on the second mission, one of which was shot down by Focquin de Grave, who was himself wounded in the stomach and forced to crash-land the D.XXI on the the Hague–Utrecht highway. The wreck of No 213 was eventually destroyed here by Dutch troops.

8

D.XXI J-47 (c/n 107) of the 2nd *Eskadrille*, Værløse, 9 April 1940

One of ten D.XXIs built by Danish Army Aviation's workshops at Copenhagen-Kløvermarken, J-47 entered service with the 2nd *Eskadrille* in early 1940, accumulating only 12 flight hours before the German invasion began. Madsen cannon were absent from its wings, armament consisting of just two 8 mm

Madsen machine guns. Danish air power was wiped out in a single attack by Bf 110s of I./ZG 1, and no D.XXI sorties were flown. J-47 was virtually destroyed, but duly rebuilt by the Danes and stored at Kløvermarken, only to be confiscated by the Germans in August 1943 and used by the Luftwaffe for second-line duties.

9
D.XXI FR-76/'Blue 3' (c/n 5438) of SSgt Mauno Fräntilä, 3/LLv 24, Lemi, March 1940
Fräntilä was a slow scorer, claiming his first aerial victory on 17 January 1940. During the Winter War he made two more claims, both as damaged. On 5 March 1940 he received hits in combat in this aeroplane and made a forced landing between the lines at Viipurinlahti. Although wounded, Fräntilä managed to escape to Finnish lines, but his aircraft was retrieved by the Red Army and exhibited as war booty in the Spartak movie theatre in Leningrad the following month. Fräntilä later flew Curtiss Hawks and Bf 109Gs, attaining a final score of 5.5 aerial victories.

10
D.XXI FR-104/'Blue 4' (c/n III/6) of 1Lt Eino Luukkanen, 3/LLv 24, Immola, December 1939
This aircraft was assigned to the leader of 3/LLv 24, 1Lt Eino Luukkanen, and on 1 December 1939 he claimed his first kill (an SB bomber of 24th SBAP) with it. He did not fly FR-104 for very long, however, as on 18 December the aeroplane was hit in the engine by flak and Luukkanen ended up with the fighter on its nose after he had force-landed it in a field. Having scored 2.5 victories in the Winter War, Luukkanen subsequently increased his tally to 54 kills while leading 1/LLv 24, LeLv 30 and LeLv 34 during the Continuation War. This score made him the third-ranking Finnish ace and earned him a Mannerheim Cross on 18 June 1944.

11
D.XXI FR-83/'Black 2' (c/n II/1) of WO Yrjö Turkka, 1/LLv 24, Lemi, March 1940
Turkka was also one of the 'old hands' of LLv 24, already holding the rank of warrant officer before the Winter War commenced. Called 'Pappa' by the junior pilots in the squadron, he set them a good example. Turkka claimed all of his 1939-40 victories in this particular fighter, being just one shared kill short of becoming an ace. All but one of his Winter War victims were bombers. He later flew Buffaloes with LeLv 24 and Bf 109Gs with both LeLvs 24 and 34. Turkka became an ace on the very first day of the Continuation War, and claiming steadily over the next two years, he was credited with his final kill (an Il-2) on 26 July 1943. This took his final tally to 17.5 victories.

12
D.XXI FR-97/'White 2' (c/n III/1) of 1Lt Jorma Sarvanto, 4/LLv 24, Utti, January 1940
Sarvanto became the first Finnish ace during a four-minute action on 6 January 1940, using this aircraft to down six DB-3Ms of 6th DBAP south of Utti. His exploits received much coverage in the international press, and 'Zamba' Sarvanto went on to become the leading ace of the Winter War. On 1 February 1940 he was made deputy leader of 1/LLv 24, and

after two victories with both FR-80 and FR-100 he had raised his score to 13 confirmed aerial kills in three weeks, becoming the top scorer in the D.XXI. Sarvanto was then posted to Sweden to evaluate the new Brewster Model 239. In the Continuation War he added four more victories in the Brewster to take his final tally to 17.

13
D.XXI FR-110/'Blue 7' (c/n III/17) of WO Viktor Pyötsiä, 3/LLv 24, Joroinen, April 1940
Serving with 3/LLv 24, Pyötsiä scored 7.5 kills in FR-110 during the Winter War, this tally including two 'doubles' on 27 December 1939 and 20 January 1940. This fighter was one of only two known examples to have carried victory symbols during the Winter War. Whether the kill markings were also applied to the port side of the fin is as yet unconfirmed. 'Isä-Vikki' ('Father Vikki') was one of the 'old hands' of LLv 24, remaining with the unit throughout the five years of conflict. During the Continuation War he served in the 1st Flight, flying Brewsters and Bf 109Gs. His final score was 21.5 confirmed aerial victories.

14
D.XXI FR-92/'Black 5' (c/n II/10) of 1Lt Per Sovelius, 4/LLv 24, Utti, January 1940
Although Maj Gustav Magnusson was LLv 24's squadron commander, he also elected to lead the 4th Flight. Sovelius was deputy leader of this flight throughout the Winter War, becoming his squadron's second-highest scorer and ending the conflict just one shared victory short of eight confirmed kills. All of his claims were made in FR-92. During the Continuation War Sovelius led 4/LLv 24 until he was assigned to air force headquarters on 19 February 1942. He ended the war one shared victory shy of being a triple ace with 14.75 kills. Promoted to the rank of major, Sovelius commanded fighter squadron HLeLv 28 in the final months of the Continuation War.

15
D.XXI FR-112/'Black 7' (c/n III/13) of 1Lt Jorma Karhunen, 1/LLv 24, Immola, December 1939
'Joppe' Karhunen flew FR-112 for five weeks while he was deputy leader of 1/LLv 24, scoring three and two shared kills during this time. His scoring run in the fighter ended on 3 January 1940 when FR-112 was damaged in a taxiing accident with another D.XXI at Värtsilä, requiring it to be sent away for repairs. Karhunen's final score with the Fokker fighter was 6.5 kills. On 30 January Karhunen was appointed commander of 2/LLv 24, although he spent the rest of the Winter War test-flying Brewsters in Sweden. During the Continuation War Karhunen commanded the 3rd Flight and, from 1 June 1943, the whole squadron, achieving a score of 31.5 victories. He was awarded the Mannerheim Cross on 8 September 1942.

16
D.XXI FR-117/'White 8' (c/n III/19) of 2Lt Olli Puhakka, 1/LLv 24, Joutseno, January 1940
This fighter was allocated to Puhakka when ten D.XXIs and pilots from LLv 26 were assigned to LLv 24 upon the latter unit's mobilisation on 23 October 1939. He claimed four

bombers destroyed in FR-117, plus one more in FR-76, thus becoming one of the 11 Winter War aces. On 2 March 1940 Puhakka was posted back to his old unit, LLv 26, which was now equipped with Fiat G.50s, where he increased his Winter War tally to seven confirmed victories. During the Continuation War he few G.50s with LeLv 26 and Bf 109Gs with LeLv 34. Puhakka's final tally reached 46 aerial victories. He received the Mannerheim Cross on 21 December 1944.

17

D.XXI FR-109/'White X' (c/n III/10) of Capt Erkki Heinilä, E/LLv 32, Utti, July 1941

During the Winter War future 22.5-victory ace WO Eero Kinnunen of 1/LLv 24 scored all of his 3.5 D.XXI kills in this aircraft. After a comprehensive overhaul at the State Aircraft Factory, FR-109 was assigned to LLv 32 commander Capt Erkki Heinilä on 28 April 1941. Heinilä was flying this aeroplane on 8 July 1941 when he shared in the destruction of a DB-3 bomber from 1st AP KBF with Cpl Mauno Kirjonen, a future ten-victory ace. Heinilä had the distinction of performing the last flight of a propeller-driven fighter in the *Ilmavoimat* on 13 March 1954 at the controls of Bf 109G-6 MT-507.

18

D.XXI FR-113/'Blue 9' (c/n III/15) of 1Lt Aulis Bremer, 2/LLv 32, Hyvinkää, June 1941

During the Winter War this aeroplane was assigned to 5/LLv 24 leader 1Lt Leo Ahola, who claimed his two aerial victories in it. After a full overhaul the fighter was assigned to 2/LLv 32 deputy leader 1Lt Aulis Bremer, who used it in the early stages of the Continuation War. When LLv 32 established a 3rd Flight on 28 June 1941 with Wasp-powered D.XXIs, Bremer was put in command and assigned FR-160. Although he did not make any claims with the D.XXI, Bremer later became a 7.5-victory ace in the same unit flying Curtiss Hawk 75As.

19

D.XXI FR-95/'White 5' (c/n II/13) of SSgt Paul Salminen, 1/LLv 32, Utti, July 1941

During the Winter War this fighter was assigned to MSgt Lars Heikinaro of 4/LLv 24, who made two claims while flying it. Having not yet been overhauled following its exertions in 1939-40, FR-95 was assigned to Salminen upon the mobilisation of the *Ilmavoimat* on 17 June 1941 in preparation for the Continuation War. As his only D.XXI claim, Salminen shared with 2Lt Alpo Lakio the destruction of a 58th SBAP Petlyakov Pe-2 bomber on 3 July 1941, flying FR-108. Later, flying Curtiss Hawk 75As, Salminen became an ace with a total of six aerial victories to his credit.

20

D.XXI FR-114/'White 2' (c/n III/21) of 1Lt Veikko Evinen, 1/LLv 32, Utti, June 1941

This aircraft was assigned to Sgt Lasse Aaltonen of 5/LLv 24 during the Winter War. He later accumulated a total of 13.5 victories flying G.50s and Bf 109Gs. After a thorough overhaul, FR-114 was then assigned to 1/LLv 32 deputy leader 1Lt Veikko Evinen, who opened his unit's account with two victories on the first day of the Continuation War, 25

June 1941, while flying FR-116. Evinen later became an ace with six victories, claimed while flying Curtiss Hawk and Bf 109G fighters. His Curtiss, CU-581, was hit by flak on 24 June 1944, and he died of wounds the following day.

21

D.XXI FR-98/'White 3' (c/n III/2) of Maj Auvo Maunula, E/LLv 12, Nurmoila, May 1942

FR-98 was a real 'ace aeroplane' of the Winter War, its pilots claiming six victories, five of them achieved by SSgt Lauri Nissinen of 5/LLv 24. After a period with LLv 32, it was transferred to reconnaissance squadron LLv 12 on 15 July 1941. Although the fighter was assigned to the 1st Flight, it was flown on several occasions by the squadron commander, Maj Maunula, who scored one of his three aerial victories in it on 19 February 1942 when he shot down an R-5 biplane. Maunula later commanded LeLv 28, but was killed in a flying accident on 17 May 1944. He had previously been awarded the Mannerheim Cross on 8 September 1942 for his exploits as a reconnaissance pilot.

22

D.XXI FR-129/'Red 1' (c/n IV/12) of Capt Veikko Karu, 2/LLv 30, Suulajärvi, November 1941

This was the most successful Wasp-powered D.XXI, being assigned to 2/LLv 30 leader 1Lt Karu on 20 March 1941. Having claimed three victories in the Winter War, Karu became the top-scoring D.XXI pilot of the Continuation War with 6.5 victories to his name, five attained in FR-129. Not only was his flight credited with 30 aerial victories, its pilots also claimed the sinking of 17 light surface vessels (patrol and motor torpedo boats). Karu's final score was one shared short of 11 aerial victories. He later commanded HLeLv 30, flying Bf 109Gs. Karu received the Mannerheim Cross on 6 November 1942.

23

D.XXI FR-125/'Red 4' (c/n IV/8) of 2Lt Ture Mattila, 2/LLv 30, Suulajärvi, October 1941

Mattila initially served in 2/LLv 30 as the wingman of Veikko Karu. On 8 July 1941 Mattila claimed a Beriev MBR flying boat destroyed during his first aerial combat, and although his aircraft's port tyre was punctured by return fire, Mattila made a safe landing at Hyvinkää. When the 1st Flight was re-established on 20 October 1941 by splitting the 25-aircraft-strong 2nd Flight, Mattila and FR-125 were posted there for a month. He later served with LeLv 34, flying Bf 109Gs and claiming four confirmed victories, which took his final score to 5.5 kills.

24

D.XXI FR-146/'Yellow 1' (c/n IV/29) of Sgt Hemmo Leino, Lentue Käär/LLv 14, Tiiksjärvi, May 1942

FR-146 served with 3/LLv 30 from the beginning of the Continuation War, this flight becoming 1/LLv 10 on 18 September 1941 and, six weeks later, *Lentue* Käär of LLv 14. Here, FR-146 was assigned to Cpl Leino, who scored 1.5 victories with it. Leino later added two kills flying MS.406s with LeLv 14 before being posted to LeLv 34 on 19 April 1943. Flying the Bf 109G with the latter unit, he took his score to 11 confirmed victories.

25
D.XXI FR-157 (c/n IV/40) of Maj Lauri Bremer, E/LLv 30, Utti, September 1941

Brand new FR-157 was assigned to LLv 30 commander Capt Bremer on 30 May 1941, just 26 days before the Continuation War commenced. The playing card motif on the fighter's rudder was unique at this stage of the war. Although Lauri Bremer (the elder brother of Aulis Bremer) did not claim any aerial victories of his own, the victory bar on the rudder denotes an MBR-2 flying boat of 58th OAE KBF that was shared with Karu (FR-129) and Mattila (FR-157) on 6 August 1941. Bremer turned this machine over while landing at Suur-Merijoki on 24 March 1942.

26
D.XXI FR-148/'Yellow 3' (s/n IV/31) of 1Lt Martti Kalima, 3/LLv 30 and Lentue Käär/LLv 14, Tiiksjärvi, March 1942

At the start of the Continuation War Kalima was deputy leader of 3/LLv 30. He scored his unit's first victory on 6 July 1941 when he downed an SB reconnaissance bomber of 117th RAE. Kalima subsequently flew with 1/LLv 10 and Lentue Käär/LLv 14, gaining four aerial victories at the controls of the D.XXI. He added another 6.5 victories to his score while flying MS.406s with LeLv 14, and eventually led the unit's 2nd Flight. His combat career came to an end on 14 June 1944 when he was posted to Germany as head of a detachment of pilots sent for nightfighter training.

27
D.XXI FR-140/'Yellow 11' (c/n IV/23) of 2Lt Esko Hyvärinen, 3/LeLv 14, Tiiksjärvi, March 1943

This D.XXI served continuously for one month short of two years, beginning on 18 May 1941 with LLv 32, moving on to LLv 30 and then, from 1 November 1941, serving with LLv 14. FR-140 had no claims to its credit, but performed well in the reconnaissance role. Its destruction came on 13 May 1943 when the aircraft was hit by rifle-calibre groundfire that killed its pilot, 2Lt Ola Tuomisto. The fighter wore the 'Yellow 11' tactical code on its rudder throughout its life. White distemper was used on D.XXIs at Tiiksjärvi during the winter of 1942-43 only.

28
D.XXI FR-156/'White 0' (c/n IV/39) of Capt Jorma Sarvanto, 2/T-LeLv 35, Kauhava, July 1944

FR-156 was the last aircraft assigned to D.XXI top-scorer Capt Jorma Sarvanto (13 confirmed aerial victories) when he was an instructor and led 2/T-LeLv 35 during the final months of the Continuation War. This aeroplane began its career on 30 May 1941 with 3/LLv 30, moving on to 1/LLv 10 and then Lentue Käär/LLv 14 on 1 November 1941. It assumed the reconnaissance role on 1 August 1942 after scoring 1.5 aerial victories, the last, an R-5 biplane, being claimed just a week before FR-156 switched from fighter-reconnaissance to reconnaissance only.

BIBLIOGRAPHY

De Jong, Peter, Fokker D.21 – Fokkers laatste eenmotorige jager, Lanasta, Netherlands, 2012

De Jong, Peter, Le Fokker D.21, Lela Presse, France, 2005

Gerdessen, Frits, Nederlandse Militaire Luchtvaart I – Fokker D-XXI (vol. 1), SVMLM, Netherlands, 1988

Gerdessen, Frits, Nederlandse Militaire Luchtvaart VI – Fokker D-XXI (vol. 2), SVMLM, Netherlands, 1991

Gerritse, Peter, De Mei-vliegers – Het persoonlijke verhaal van frontpiloot Jan Linzel, Bosch & Keuning, Netherlands, 1995

Hooftman, Hugo, Nederlandse Luchtvaartenyclopedie (vol. 5) – Fokker D.XXI, Cockpit-Uitgeverij, Netherlands, 1978

Juutilainen, Ilmari, Double Fighter Knight, Apali Oy, Finland, 1996

Luukkanen, Eino, Fighter over Finland, Macdonald, England, 1963

Stenman, Kari, 'First and last – Finnish Fokker D.XXIs', Air Enthusiast No 88, Key Publishing, England, 2000

Stenman, Kari and Keskinen, Kalevi, Osprey Aircraft of the Aces 23 - Finnish Fighter Aces of World War 2, Osprey Publishing, England, 1998

Stenman, Kari and Keskinen, Kalevi, Osprey Aviation Elite 4 - Lentolaivue 24, Osprey Publishing, England, 2001

Van Overvest, H J, 'Last of the fighting Fokkers – flying the D.XXI', Air International, England, October 1977

INDEX